seventeen's

guide to
getting into
college

know yourself,
know your schools
& find your perfect fit!

JAYE J. FENDERSON

HEARST BOOKS

A division of Sterling Publishing Co., Inc.

New York / London
www.sterlingpublishing.com

Book design by Kelly Roberts

Library of Congress Cataloging-in-Publication Data
Fenderson, Jaye J.
Seventeen's guide to getting into college / Jaye J. Fenderson.
p. cm.
Includes bibliographical references and index.
ISBN-13: 978-1-58816-647-0
1. Universities and colleges—United States—Admission—Juvenile literature. I. Seventeen. II. Title. III. Title: Guide to getting into college.
LB2351.2.F46 2008
378.1'610973—dc22
2007034032

10 9 8 7 6 5 4 3 2 1

Published by Hearst Books
A Division of Sterling Publishing Co., Inc.
387 Park Avenue South, New York, NY 10016

www.seventeen.com

For information about custom editions, special sales, premium and corporate purchases, please contact Sterling Special Sales Department at 800-805-5489 or specialsales@sterlingpublishing.com.

Distributed in Canada by Sterling Publishing
℅ Canadian Manda Group, 165 Dufferin Street
Toronto, Ontario, Canada M6K 3H6

Distributed in Australia by Capricorn Link (Australia) Pty. Ltd.
P.O. Box 704, Windsor, NSW 2756 Australia

Manufactured in China

Sterling ISBN: 978-1-58816-647-0

contents

hi!

So you probably picked up this book because you're either freaking out about applying to college, or you're so excited about the next phase of your life that you can't wait to get started (probably a little of both!). I didn't always know that I wanted to be in the magazine business: When I was applying to colleges, I was convinced that I'd have a great career as a novelist! At first, I wasn't sure what kind of school would be right for me—big university or small liberal-arts college? Busy city school or a beautiful college campus? I applied to half a dozen schools and wrote draft after draft of my college essay. But it didn't take long for me to find the perfect school—New York University—a big school in the middle of the busiest city in the U.S. I was in HEAVEN!

Even if you have no idea where you want to go to school or what you want to major in, it's never too early to start laying the groundwork. We wrote this book to help you figure out where you want to be in life—and get there! Everyone has a different path to their big future. Don't worry: everyone gets that sick feeling when they look through blind college listings. And everyone gets nervous about what their grades and test scores mean. We want you to understand all the ins and outs of the college application process and this book will show you what's worth spending time getting right, and what's not really worth sweating over. Plus, *Seventeen* can't help but make the whole process FUN too!

This is the first step toward your future—getting into the right college for you. Thanks for taking it with us...and don't forget, we'll always be here for you whenever you need us.

Ann Shoket, *Seventeen* editor-in-chief

introduction

Choosing a college can be a totally thrilling experience. It's like shopping for a whole new life out of a mail order catalog! As the brochures start filling your mailbox, you start imagining all the new friends you'll have, your sweet (sibling-free) dorm room, parties with no curfew, classes that don't instantly put you to sleep, and of course, the fabulous future that comes along with your degree.

Then the panic sets in. What if you don't pick the right school? What if you don't get in? What if your parents say you can't afford it? Between the test prep books, the application forms, the looming deadlines and all the well-meaning advice everyone keeps throwing at you, choosing a college can also be a totally *stressful* experience.

That's where this book comes in. We're here to give you the inside edge—that extra info you need to sail through your applications without suffering a nervous breakdown and to get accepted at the perfect school for *you*. Whether you have your sights set on the Ivy League or the local community college, getting there doesn't have to make you nuts. You might be a freshman getting a head start on things or a senior scrambling to get your applications sent off by January 1; either way, we'll give you a game plan for sorting out your options, impressing the people who'll decide your fate, and staying on track with dates and deadlines. Along the way, you'll get tons of tricks and secrets straight from admissions officers who can prepare you for applying like no one else.

Most importantly, we'll show you *how to tell your story.* Because that's what applying to college is all about. Behind your grades and test scores, you're a person with experiences that have already begun to shape who you'll become. And when colleges get to know you, it's easier for them to figure out if they can help shape the rest of your life. In fact, before you can even begin to think about where to go to school or how to fill out those intimidating questionnaires, you need to figure out what exactly your story is, because if you don't, you're going to have a hard time explaining it to someone else. So, consider this book your one-stop shop for finding—and being accepted at—the school that will best help *you* grow into the person you want to be.

calendar

FRESHMAN YEAR

The choices you make in ninth, tenth, and eleventh grades will determine what kind of colleges you'll be able to get into. So the sooner you realize you want to go to college, the sooner you can begin researching schools that will be a good fit for you, finding out each one's requirements or recommendations for admission, and then planning your classes and activities around those.

This four-year calendar will help you map out everything you need to do. Our recommendations are listed on the side (you'll find how-to info on all of them throughout the book), and you can fill in the blanks with any additional dates and deadlines.

myth Junior and senior years are when all the college-planning stuff happens.

truth The earlier you start preparing, the more options you'll have and the less stressed out you'll be by the time your senior year rolls around.

- Start reading about colleges in guidebooks or online.
- Make nice with at least one or two of your teachers and stay in touch with them (you might need them later on for recommendations!).
- Sign up for electives that truly interest you (not necessarily the same old ones you've always taken).
- Enroll in a foreign language class (most colleges require at least two or three years).
- Try out different clubs and activities to see which ones you really like (you can drop the duds next year!).

17 FYI

Colleges consider your grades from all _four_ years when deciding whether to admit you. Keep that in mind when you're thinking about blowing off homework!

freshman calendar

fall

winter

spring

summer

SOPHOMORE YEAR

- Over the summer, get into the habit of reading a few unassigned books each year about topics that interest you. (If romance novels are what interest you—so be it! Maybe you'll become a fiction writer...)

- Find out what honors, AP, or upper level classes your high school offers and ask your guidance counselor if you're eligible for them.

- Meet with your guidance counselor to fill her in on your plans for the future.

17 TIP

If you haven't yet, now is the time to enroll in a foreign language class. Already took one year? Sign up for a second: Strangely enough, it can help with your English vocab on the SAT.

- If there's something you enjoy doing and no club for it, ask your favorite teacher to help you start one. (Admissions officers go nuts for that kind of initiative!)

- Pick the club or activity you like most and volunteer to head up a special project—colleges love leaders!

- If you want to get a head start preparing for the SAT and ACT, sign up now to take the PSAT/NMSQT or PLAN in the fall of your junior year.

sophomore calendar

fall

winter

spring

summer

JUNIOR YEAR

- Buy a college guidebook or start logging some serious time with an online guide.

- Make a short list of subjects you might want to major in, then research which schools offer the best programs in those fields. (You can always change your mind later.)

- Choose a favorite activity and run for a leadership office (like president or secretary) at the next annual election.

- Start building a list of favorite colleges to focus your research on.

- Beef up your schedule with honors or AP classes, if possible, even just in elective classes like art if they're offered. (You might find they're not that much harder than regular classes!)

- Take the PSAT/NMSQT in the fall.

- Schedule campus visits for this spring, summer, or next fall.

- Plan your senior year classes.

17 FYI
Junior year grades often weigh more heavily in admissions officers' minds than those from the last two years. So keep up the good work!

- Take the SAT and/or ACT in the spring.

- Sign up for SAT Subject Tests and/or AP tests.

- Start researching scholarships from outside companies and organizations.

- Ask your parents about the family financial situation and make a tuition budget.

Turn the page to see your calendar!

junior calendar

fall

winter

junior calendar

spring

summer

SENIOR YEAR

- Focus your time and energy on the extracurriculars that are the most important to you (that's *you*—not your mom, or your best friend, or your coach). Propose a new project or goal to take on, then head up the effort.

- Fill out the College Scholarship Service Profile when it becomes available after September 1.

- Narrow your list to eight or ten schools that you'll apply to, and decide whether to apply "early admission" to any of them.

- Start a file for each of your schools where you'll keep all brochures, application materials, and correspondence.

- Mark all deadlines and requirements on this calendar!

- Start brainstorming specific essay topics as soon as applications are available.

- Find out if interviews are required by your schools and when you can expect to be contacted for one.

- Sign up for fall SAT or ACT dates.

- Take any SAT Subject Tests required by your schools.

- Report required test scores to your schools. You can send your scores to up to four schools in a single test sitting. To send more scores, you must wait until you receive your results. Then you can send your scores online for an additional fee.

- Meet with teachers to ask them for recommendation letters. Hand them (and your guidance counselor) any forms they'll need by early fall.

- Meet with your guidance counselor at least a month before your first application deadline to make sure you're both on track to get everything submitted on time.

- Start writing your essays and filling in your applications.

- Check in with the teachers who are writing your recommendations a week before the letters are due.

- Make sure you've gathered all the extra stuff you need to submit along with your applications (like an art portfolio, recommendation letters, etc.).

- Proofread your entire application and ask a friend or teacher to do the same.

- Make photocopies of paper applications and print out online applications.

- Submit your applications!

- Send each of the people who wrote you a recommendation letter a thank you note.

17 FYI

Colleges can and do take back acceptance offers in cases of severe senioritis! Keep up with your classes even after you've gotten in.

- If you're applying for financial aid, complete the FAFSA as soon as possible after January 1, along with any additional financial aid forms.

- Compare financial aid packages from schools that admit you.

- Plan spring visits to schools that admit you to help you make your final decision.

- Accept an offer of admission and send in your deposit.

- Take any senior year AP exams (you won't need them to get in at this point, but they might get you out of certain 101-level college courses).

- Make plans for a well-deserved summer vacation!

Turn the page to see your calendar!

senior calendar

september

october

november

december

senior calendar

january

february

march

april

may

This book is a little different from all the other college guidebooks out there, so here's how it works:

Calendar

At the front of the book is a master four-year calendar, and it's blank on purpose, so that you can fill in the dates and deadlines that correspond to your schedule. Don't worry about filling in all four years if you're a senior, junior, or sophomore—just start wherever you are in the admissions process. For seventh- and eighth-graders, it's a good idea to get in the habit now of keeping track of key dates, but you don't need to begin using these calendars until you start high school.

Pocket Organizers

Each chapter has a pocket folder to help you keep track of college brochures, financial aid info, essay ideas, resumes, accomplishments, awards, and anything else you collect during your search.

17 Reader Advice

Scattered throughout each chapter are tips from girls like you who are currently going through or have already been through the college admissions process. Go ahead and steal their strategies or learn from their mistakes—they don't mind!

Fun Stuff

You'll find all sorts of interactive exercises in each chapter that will help you take all the important info in the book and apply it to your life.

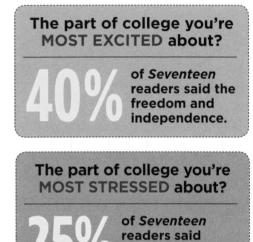

The part of college you're MOST EXCITED about?

40% of *Seventeen* readers said the freedom and independence.

The part of college you're MOST STRESSED about?

25% of *Seventeen* readers said the cost.

Now grab a pen, take a deep breath, and get ready to start planning your new life!

For the first time ever, **you're the one in control of where your life is headed**: where you'll live, what you'll study, and, equally important, what you'll do when you're not studying. So obviously you want to **make the right choice** for you. The way to do that is to really **get to know yourself**—your likes, dislikes, strengths and weaknesses. Once you've got those down, you'll be able to **pick the schools** where you'll do best and be happiest. *And* you'll be able to convince admissions counselors that you belong there.

THE BASIC PROCESS GOES LIKE THIS:

step 1
figure out your talents and abilities

step 2
understand your personality

step 3
find a way to make the most of your skills

"Who am I?"

It seems like a simple enough question, but it actually takes some soul-searching to answer well. It's easy to get so focused on what you want that you don't bother to figure out whether or not your goals make sense in light of who you are. You want to ace the exam, make the team, get the guy, win the election, get into the school of your dreams (or all of the above). But if you haven't stopped to consider whether your desires and abilities match up, you could be setting yourself up for major disappointment. Getting a clear sense of your identity, talents, and abilities will help you figure out where to set your sights in life—and answer the "who am I?" question throughout your college applications.

Start by creating a character sketch. It's something authors and filmmakers use to spell out a character's background and the motivations behind her actions in the story. When it comes to telling your story to an admissions officer—either in your applications or in person—it helps to write up a sketch of the heroine. That'd be you.

College applications are all about describing how past experiences, activities, and accomplishments have resulted in the person you are today. That's a huge question, so start with what you know—take time to answer the following smaller questions honestly and thoughtfully. They'll help you get closer to the big picture.

character sketch

1 Draw a family tree in the space provided, listing yourself, your parents, siblings, and any other significant family members. Next to each one, write his or her name, age, occupation, and a one-word personality description.

2 Describe your immediate family. What role do you think you play in your family? Do you feel positively or negatively toward your family and why?

_____
_____
_____
_____
_____

3 List the places you have lived and the number of years in each place.

_____
_____
_____
_____

4 Describe your hometown. Do you feel positively or negatively toward it and why?

_____
_____
_____
_____

5 What is your favorite memory from childhood ?

_____
_____
_____
_____

6 When you were younger, what did you want to be when you grew up? How have your thoughts changed since then?

_____

_____

_____

_____

7 List your favorite childhood heroes, books, cartoons, movies, and toys.

_____

_____

_____

_____

8 What are your hobbies? What do you like to do for fun?

_____

_____

_____

_____

9 How would your best friend describe your personality?

_____

_____

_____

_____

10 What would your worst enemy say about you?

_____

_____

_____

11 How have you changed from when you were in elementary school and junior high?

_____

_____

_____

_____

12 What is the one thing you are the most proud of in your life and why?

_____

_____

_____

_____

13 If you were stranded on a desert island, what three things would you want to take with you? Explain the significance of each one.

_____

_____

_____

_____

17 TIP

Take an inventory of your room. What elements are most important to you—your music collection, clothes, posters, books, memorabilia? Why are they significant? Can you find a common theme to the objects that decorate your walls, line your shelves, or fill up your desk? What does your style say about your personality?

14 What are your best qualities?
Your worst qualities?

_____

_____

_____

_____

15 Whose opinion matters to you most
and why?

_____

_____

_____

_____

16 If you could change one thing about
yourself, what would it be?

_____

_____

_____

_____

17 Where would you like to be in
ten years? Twenty years?

_____

_____

_____

_____

Okay, so now you have your character sketch. Take a look at your answers. Do you see any patterns developing? Does anything surprise you? The questions are meant to help you gain perspective on your past, present, and future, and what's important to you. You can look back at this page whenever you feel like your story isn't going anywhere. And, remember, you're constantly evolving and discovering new things about yourself, so make changes to your sketch as needed.

finding your talents

SKILLS LIST: Check off all talents that apply to you. Look closely: Even if you don't have *formal* experience in an area, you might still have natural ability in it. Like, if you decorated your room, and everyone always says it looks awesome—that's interior design! When you're done, narrow down the list to the top five skills you'd like to pursue further, and, in the space provided, write down examples of how you've used those skills in your life so far.

- ○ Accounting
- ○ Acting
- ○ Athletic talent
- ○ Auto mechanics
- ○ Blogging
- ○ Caring for sick
- ○ Carpentry
- ○ Closing a sale
- ○ Coaching
- ○ Collaborative projects
- ○ Comedy
- ○ Completing tasks
- ○ Conflict mediation
- ○ Cooking
- ○ Coordinating activities
- ○ Counseling
- ○ Creative writing
- ○ Dancing
- ○ Data analysis
- ○ Debating
- ○ Directing theater or film
- ○ Drawing
- ○ Editing and writing
- ○ Emceeing

- ○ Environmental awareness
- ○ Fashion design
- ○ Finding a bargain
- ○ Fixing things
- ○ Gardening
- ○ Graphic design
- ○ Handling a crisis
- ○ Healthy living
- ○ Hosting events
- ○ Improvisation
- ○ Information sciences
- ○ Interior design
- ○ Languages
- ○ Leadership
- ○ Literary analysis
- ○ Marketing/Publicity
- ○ Math
- ○ Multitasking
- ○ Mentoring
- ○ Negotiating
- ○ Observational skills
- ○ Open to new ideas
- ○ Overseeing projects
- ○ Outdoor adventures

- ○ Painting
- ○ Party planning
- ○ Paying attention to details
- ○ Photography
- ○ Playing an instrument
- ○ Political organization
- ○ Problem solving
- ○ Product design and invention
- ○ Public speaking
- ○ Research
- ○ Scientific studies
- ○ Sculpture
- ○ Setting goals
- ○ Sewing
- ○ Singing
- ○ Storytelling
- ○ Teaching
- ○ Traveling
- ○ Understanding how things work
- ○ Working with animals
- ○ Working with elderly
- ○ Working with kids

TOP FIVE SKILLS	HOW I USE EACH SKILL
1	
2	
3	
4	
5	

K nowing your background, talents, and abilities is just part of the puzzle of who you are. Now you need to figure out how your skills complement your unique personality. Read the statements on the personality quiz that follows and the statement in each box that best describes you. You may find that more than one statement applies to you, but you still have to narrow it down to a single answer. Be honest! There are no "right" answers—this is just another way to help you figure out what makes you tick.

QUIZ

For each question, circle the letter of the statement that BEST describes you. Using the key on the next page, tally your answers and then check to see what your answers mean.

1
a I have incredible willpower.
b I pay attention to what others think of me.
c I don't mind doing people a favor.
d I'm known for being cheerful.

2
a I can chat for hours.
b Other people's feelings can be more important than my own.
c Traditions are important to me.
d I make decisions easily.

3
a I follow instructions easily.
b I'm very organized.
c I don't care what other people think of me.
d I like to party.

4
a I make decisions very carefully.
b I know what I want.
c I'm good at convincing other people to see things my way.
d I'm very friendly.

5
a It's hard for me to relax.
b I have tons of friends.
c I love helping people.
d I like to do the right thing.

6
a I don't like breaking the rules.
b If I know something needs to get done, I'll do it.
c I'm very loyal.
d I'm very charming.

7
a I forgive other people easily.
b I tend to take things personally.
c I have tons of energy.
d I get along with everyone.

8
a Self-control isn't a problem for me.
b I enjoy giving to others.
c I enjoy being active.
d I keep working until I accomplish my goals.

9
a I go after what I want.
b I love to have fun.
c I'm a good shoulder to cry on.
d I have a tendency to be shy.

10
a My room is super neat.
b I'm good at multitasking.
c I don't get stressed easily.
d I'm notorious for getting my way.

11
a I respect people in charge.
b I love trying new things.
c I have a super positive outlook.
d Helping others makes me happy.

12
a I keep an open mind.
b I like to debate.
c I'm very laid-back.
d I believe my dreams will come true.

13
a I love hosting parties.
b I'm a good listener.
c I can handle any situation.
d I tend not to get riled up.

14
a I like to be in charge.
b I like knowing all the facts before I make a decision.
c I always know the right thing to say.
d I'm very balanced.

15
a My friends know they can count on me.
b I love adventure.
c I avoid conflict.
d I'm very driven.

16
a I'm a fierce competitor.
b I take life in stride.
c My friends often come to me for advice.
d I tend to be practical.

17
a I'm good at persuading others.
b I'm very encouraging.
c I pay attention to details.
d I'm always doing something new and exciting.

Turn the page to find out your score!

ANSWER KEY

1a—G	7a—B	13a—S
1b—T	7b—T	13b—B
1c—B	7c—G	13c—G
1d—S	7d—S	13d—T
2a—S	8a—T	14a—G
2b—B	8b—B	14b—T
2c—T	8c—S	14c—S
2d—G	8d—G	14d—B
3a—B	9a—G	15a—B
3b—T	9b—S	15b—S
3c—G	9c—B	15c—T
3d—S	9d—T	15d—G
4a—T	10a—T	16a—G
4b—G	10b—G	16b—S
4c—S	10c—B	16c—B
4d—B	10d—S	16d—T
5a—G	11a—T	17a—S
5b—S	11b—G	17b—B
5c—B	11c—S	17c—T
5d—T	11d—B	17d—G
6a—T	12a—T	
6b—G	12b—G	
6c—B	12c—B	
6d—S	12d—S	

ADD UP YOUR TOTALS

total number of Gs _____

total number of Ss _____

total number of Bs _____

total number of Ts _____

If you picked MOSTLY Gs you're a...

go-getter

You're a leader who loves to take charge and always has creative ideas for solving problems. You don't go down without a fight and won't let obstacles stand in the way of achieving your goals.

If you picked MOSTLY Ss you're a...

social star

You're super outgoing and always up for a good time. Willing to take risks and meet new people, you're the life of the party and you fill your calendar with tons of activities.

If you picked MOSTLY Bs you're a...

best friend

You're extremely loyal. People can always count on you for an encouraging hug or special favor. You love spending time with friends and family and go the extra mile to make others happy.

If you picked MOSTLY Ts you're a...

thinker

You love it when a good plan comes together! Organized and detail-oriented, you like to have all the facts before making a decision. You see the reason behind the rules and usually choose to follow them.

Figuring out what you love to do and what you're great at doing can open up the door for you to achieve more than you ever thought possible. All you have to do now is polish your skills and figure out how to put them to good use. And the perfect place for that is in college!

Applying to college is so exciting because the **options are nearly limitless** and anything is possible. But it can also be really overwhelming if you don't know what you're looking for or what you want to get out of the experience. The most important thing to remember is that **this decision is all about you**. It's *your* education, *your* future, and *your* time to explore what you can offer the world. There isn't a perfect school out there, but you can find the perfect schools for *you*—yes, there are more than one!—if you take the time to shop around. That's why you just did all that work getting to know yourself in Chapter 1. Now you can take that info and use it to find the **best college matches for you**.

In the past, making a college choice was a little simpler. Lots of kids applied only to schools that made it into the top ten of some prestigious ranking list, or only to in-state schools because they thought that was all they could afford, or only to the school where their parents went. But today, guidance counselors and admissions officers realize how important it is to be good matchmakers. When the people and programs at a school bring out the best in you, and you bring your special talents and ideas, everybody's happy.

Just like with the romantic kind of matchmaking, finding the one you click with is as much about figuring out what you don't want as it is about knowing what you do want. With guys, you do that by dating around. You might end up kissing a few duds, but each one teaches you a little more about what you're looking for. With colleges, you do this by researching. We're willing to bet it won't be as much fun as flirting at parties (if it is, you're definitely with the wrong guys). But you might actually get into it—kind of like getting hooked on reading guys' MySpace pages and deciding whether you want to hang out with them more.

The more hours you put into research, the better your chances of discovering that perfect match. If you've ever done a college search on the web or tried to lift the huge college guidebooks at Barnes & Noble, you know there's a *lot* to choose from. Almost makes you want to just close your eyes, point to one, and be done with it. (But you probably shouldn't.) There are over 3,500 schools in the United States alone, and that means the odds are in your favor that you'll find at least a handful of schools that will make you happy.

No matter where you are in the process, the research tips in this chapter can help you figure out where to apply. There are tons of different kinds of schools, so it helps to break them down by four basic criteria: academic programs, location, size, and lifestyle.

academic programs

TYPES OF SCHOOLS

universities are institutions of higher learning that consist of an undergraduate program plus graduate schools and professional schools (medicine, law, business, and the like). A university awards both graduate degrees (masters and doctorate) and undergraduate degrees (bachelor of arts and bachelor of sciences) and tends to be larger and more research-oriented (that is, the professors split their time between teaching and conducting research studies in their subject areas).

colleges are usually smaller than universities, and they focus on undergraduate education. Liberal arts colleges offer a more traditional and general education in subjects such as literature, history, mathematics, natural science, social science, language, art, and music. Colleges that don't refer to themselves as "liberal arts" schools offer more specialized majors linked to specific careers, such as journalism, marketing, business, or nursing.

myth You should always choose the highest ranked school you can get into.

truth The *best* education is one that maximizes your potential. You want a school to meet your unique needs, and you can't make that call without knowing more than a college's ranking or reputation.

Colleges and universities can be further broken down into even more categories, like public, private, Ivy League, women's, religiously affiliated, and historically black institutions. For websites with more information about each of these categories, check out the **Resources** (page 138).

public schools get financial support from the state in which they're located. They often offer less expensive tuition to students who live in that state when they apply, and may accept more in-state applicants than out-of-state applicants.

private schools don't receive money from the state. There's a major misconception out there that private schools are automatically more expensive than publics, but that's not necessarily true, especially if you're applying to public schools outside your state. Don't rule out private schools before comparing actual price tags. To get more advice on affording college check out Chapter 8 (page 107).

the ivy league originally referred to an athletic league of eight schools: Brown, Columbia, Cornell,

Dartmouth, Harvard, Princeton, University of Pennsylvania, and Yale. Today these schools are considered prestigious and ultra competitive when it comes to g etting in. Same goes for many other highly-selective—but not technically "Ivy League"— schools, including Amherst, Duke, MIT, Stanford, University of California at Berkeley, University of Chicago, University of Virginia, and Wesleyan. If an elite school appeals to you, make sure you also research similar but less competitive universities, since pinning all your hopes on one of these top schools can be risky.

women's colleges like Barnard, Scripps, Spelman, and Wellesley have played a historic role in advancing the education of our gender. If you're hoping for an supportive and women-centered environment,

then a single-sex college may be right for you.

religiously affiliated schools weave a certain faith into their academics and campus life, but you don't always have to subscribe to that faith in order to attend. Such schools include Brandeis, Gonzaga, and Wheaton.

historically black colleges like Howard, Spelman, and Tuskegee offer top-notch educations while focusing on the needs and perspectives of the African-American student.

17 FYI

Don't judge schools by their names only: Boston College is actually a university that retained its old school name. Same for the College of William and Mary and Dartmouth College.

MORE TYPES OF SCHOOLS

art, conservatory, and design schools offer two- or four-year degrees (bachelor or associate) in areas like drawing, music, fashion, dance, theater, architecture, and photography. These very specialized courses of study often require an audition or portfolio in order to be considered for admission.

community or technical colleges offer two-year programs or associate degrees at a lower cost. Afterward, you can often transfer those credits toward a four-year degree at a university or liberal arts college, or immediately enter the workforce with practical training in fields like health or technology.

vocational or trade schools offer hands-on training and certification in a particular field or occupation, such as automotive services, cosmetology, culinary arts, or information technology. The programs can last anywhere from several weeks to a few years, eventually earning you an associate degree.

MAJORS

When researching schools, browse through the course catalogs to see what departments or classes spark your interest and only consider colleges that offer several majors that appeal to you. But remember, even if right now you have your heart set on one particular major, there's a chance you may change your mind once you get to campus. So be sure to pick schools that intrigue you for more than just the classes they offer. Use the **College Inventory** (see page 38) to help you narrow down your interests.

myth I need to declare a major on my college application or I'll look like I don't have direction or focus.

truth You don't need to decide your major or what you want to study until you get to college. But if you're totally ahead of the game and know right now that you want to study fashion merchandising or astrophysics or child developmental psychology, then you need to make sure the schools you're considering have those programs.

ACADEMIC COMPATIBILITY

You'll want to find a school where the classes don't leave you feeling bored—or in over your head. So it's important to consider the statistics. Compare your grades and test scores to the average students admitted to each school in which you are interested.

dream schools
colleges where your test scores and grades are the same as or just below those of the average admitted student.

competitive schools
colleges where your grades and test scores fall above or solidly within the range given for the average admitted student.

safety schools
colleges where your grades and test scores are well above those of the average student admitted.

17 FYI
Every school publishes the previous year's admissions data—median test scores, GPA, and more as part of the previous year's "freshman profile"—and knowing how you stack up with the competition will help you make a realistic list of colleges to apply to.

LOCATION

The three main aspects to think about are climate and geography, neighborhood, and distance from home. But don't just rely on those pretty brochures to get an accurate picture of a school's campus. Colleges put their best faces forward in marketing materials, so first figure out what's important to you and then do the research to find who's got it.

climate & geography:
Do you live in flip-flops and own a pair of sunglasses for every day of the week? Or do you love the cozy comfort of hot cocoa on a cold winter day? It's important to find out what the weather will be like from September to May, since your sunny summer visit may not represent an average day during the school year. Consider whether six inches of snow or 90-degree temps would kill your motivation to get to class every morning.

As for geography, think about your idea of the perfect study break. A long walk on the beach, a rock-climbing adventure, a visit to a museum, or dinner and a movie? Are there any particular outdoor activities that are an important part of your life—running, snowboarding, surfing, bicycling, horseback riding, hiking, ice skating, rollerblading? Find out if the local terrain works for your sport. How you want to spend your time outside the classroom will help you determine the perfect backdrop (beach, mountain, city, country) for the next four years of your life.

neighborhood:
Whether it's urban, rural, or suburban, the community surrounding a campus helps determine the overall vibe of the school. What kinds of resources—shopping, restaurants, nightlife—are available nearby? Will you feel safe? Is there enough happening on- and off-campus, or will you be bored on the weekends? Will you need to bring your car or bike to college or can you rely on public transportation? Asking yourself these questions as you research schools will help you figure out which neighborhoods suit you best.

distance from home:
Another factor you'll need to consider is how close to your family you want to be. Do you want to live at home and commute or be close enough to drive home on the weekends to do your laundry? Or do you want to experience an entirely new region, even if it means you only make it home for the holidays? Note each school's distance and consider how often you'll want to make that six-hour drive or three-hour flight—and whether you'll be able to *afford* to do so.

size does matter

There's a wide range of campus sizes to consider and each has pros and cons, but they can pretty much be broken down into S, M, and L.

UNDERGRAD POPULATION	PROS	CONS
Small (under 2,500 students)	▪ Low student/teacher ratio; get to know your profs easily in small classes ▪ Easy to get involved in campus organizations ▪ Everyone knows everyone	▪ Not as much diversity as a larger school ▪ Fewer opportunities for research, study abroad, or specialized majors ▪ Everyone knows everyone
Medium (2,500– 7,500 students)	▪ Still small enough to establish relationships with professors ▪ More majors and specializations available than at a smaller school ▪ More diversity of organizations, courses, and student body	▪ Academic advising system probably not as focused as at a smaller school ▪ Larger class sizes ▪ Some classes may be taught by graduate students rather than profs
Large (7,500+ students)	▪ Great diversity of majors, activities, special programs, and student body ▪ Possibility of major stadium sporting events ▪ Access to more research facilities and bigger libraries	▪ Large class sizes and little or no interaction with professors or graduate student instructors ▪ Potential for frustrating big-school bureaucracy ▪ Stiff competition for coveted internships or research positions

campus lifestyle

Colleges, like people, have unique personalities, so take some time to get to know the reputation of the schools in which you're interested. You're going to learn a lot outside, as well as inside, the classroom. So choose schools where you can really see yourself getting involved, making friends, and having an impact on campus. Some schools are known for their sports teams, where games are televised, the students are superspirited, and the social scene revolves around that week's athletic event. Other campuses are big into political and social activism. Some schools identify themselves with a particular religious, cultural, or ethnic group. Some are world-renowned for theater or music performances. And many are known for the strength of their Greek life—that is, their fraternities and sororities.

GOING GREEK

All schools with sororities have slightly different policies for how and when girls are selected to join. But typically there will be a "rush week," which gives prospective sisters the chance to visit the different houses, meet the members, and get to know the basics of each group (what they stand for, their role on campus, etc). Once rush is over, girls decide which houses they'd be interested in joining, and the sororities discuss whom they'd like to invite to join—hopefully resulting in a match.

At a large school, joining a sorority can be a big help, since it's often easier to make friends within a smaller community—you'll have a built-in resource of older girls you can go to for advice or support. Sororities are also known for organizing lots of parties, formal dances, and charity events, so if you're into those things too, it can be a great opportunity to meet other like-minded girls. And your social calendar will always be full!

Going Greek can be a huge time and money commitment; if you do rush, be sure to ask each house what kind of cash you'll need (beyond regular dues) so that you know what you're getting into before you join. Along with the expense, another drawback is that belonging to a house can sometimes make it difficult to meet people or do activities outside your sorority, because of the time commitment.

TAKE THIS WITH YOU!

COLLEGE REPORT CARD

You aren't the only one being evaluated during the long application process; the schools are being judged too—by you. Make copies of this worksheet and bring it along on campus visits to see which colleges make your grade.

Accessibility of Professors	A B C D F	Libraries	A B C D F
Advising System	A B C D F	Location	A B C D F
Average Class Size	A B C D F	Nearby Restaurants	A B C D F
Campus Grounds	A B C D F	Nearby Shopping	A B C D F
Campus Neighborhood	A B C D F	Off-campus Activities	A B C D F
Dining Hall	A B C D F	School Spirit	A B C D F
Dorm Bathrooms	A B C D F	Strength of Academics	A B C D F
Dorm Rooms	A B C D F	Variety of Campus Activities	A B C D F
Food	A B C D F	Variety of Majors	A B C D F
Greek Life	A B C D F	Vibe of Students	A B C D F
Gym	A B C D F	**OVERALL GRADE**	**A B C D F**

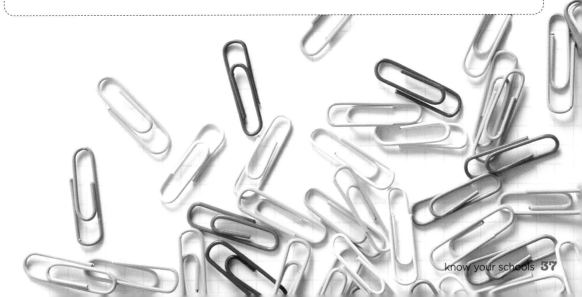

PUTTING IT ALL TOGETHER

Use the College Inventory below to check off your preferences and the activities and organizations that spark your interest. Then keep these factors in mind when deciding whether schools are a good fit for you.

college inventory

Check off the items in each section that are important or interesting to you. Then use this chart as you do your research.

size

○ Small (under 2,500)   ○ Medium (2,500-7,500)   ○ Large (7,500+)

locations

DISTANCE FROM HOME
○ In the same town   ○ 1–2 hours driving distance   ○ 5–10 hours driving distance
○ A plane flight away   ○ Distance doesn't matter

WEATHER
○ Sunny all the time   ○ Winter wonderland   ○ Changing seasons   ○ Rainy but green

GEOGRAPHY & NEIGHBORHOODS
○ Mountains   ○ Beaches   ○ City   ○ Country   ○ Suburban

majors & programs of study

ENGINEERING
○ Aerospace Engineering   ○ Architecture   ○ Biomedical Engineering
○ Computer Science   ○ Electrical Engineering   ○ Mechanical Engineering

BUSINESS/COMMUNICATIONS
○ Accounting   ○ Advertising   ○ Business   ○ Communications   ○ Economics
○ Finance   ○ Graphic Design   ○ Journalism   ○ Marketing   ○ Public Relations

HUMANITIES
○ Art   ○ Art History   ○ Classics   ○ Creative Writing   ○ Dance   ○ English
○ Film   ○ Foreign Languages   ○ History   ○ Music   ○ Philosophy   ○ Theater

INTERDISCIPLINARY STUDIES
○ Ethnic and Cultural Studies   ○ Criminal Justice and Law   ○ Environmental Studies
○ International Relations   ○ Religious Studies   ○ Urban Studies   ○ Women's Studies

LIFE AND PHYSICAL SCIENCES
○ Agriculture ○ Astronomy ○ Biology ○ Botany ○ Chemistry ○ Geology
○ Marine Biology ○ Math ○ Medicine ○ Nursing ○ Nutrition ○ Physics
○ Statistics ○ Veterinary Science ○ Zoology

SOCIAL SCIENCES
○ Anthropology ○ Archaeology ○ Education ○ Forensic Science ○ Linguistics
○ Political Science ○ Psychology ○ Social Work ○ Sociology

VOCATIONAL STUDIES
○ Cosmetology ○ Culinary Arts ○ Fashion Design ○ Hospitality
○ Hotel Management ○ Interior Design ○ Landscaping ○ Restaurant Management

LIST ADDITIONAL MAJORS OF INTEREST HERE:

_____
_____
_____

activities, clubs, athletics

○ Amnesty International ○ Anime Club ○ Archery ○ Art Shows ○ Basketball
○ Bowling ○ Cheerleading ○ Chess Club ○ Choir ○ Coffeehouse ○ Concerts
○ Culinary Society ○ Cultural Groups ○ Dance ○ Debate ○ Extreme Sports
○ Film Production/Society ○ Gay and Lesbian Groups ○ Greek Life ○ Gymnastics
○ Hiking ○ Hockey ○ Ice Skating ○ Improv/Sketch Comedy ○ Instrumental Music
○ Intramural Sports ○ Lacrosse ○ Language Clubs ○ Literary Magazine
○ Marching Band ○ Mock Trial ○ Model Congress ○ Model United Nations
○ Newspaper ○ Peer Counseling ○ Political Organizations ○ Publications
○ Quiz Bowl ○ Rock Climbing ○ Rowing ○ Radio ○ Religious Groups ○ Sailing
○ Service Organizations ○ Skiing/Snowboarding ○ Slam Poetry ○ Soccer
○ Softball ○ Student Government ○ Study Abroad ○ Swimming ○ Television
○ Tennis ○ Theater ○ Track ○ Ultimate Frisbee ○ Unicef ○ Women's Groups

LIST ADDITIONAL ACTIVITIES OF INTEREST HERE:

_____
_____
_____
_____
_____
_____

how to research schools

IN BOOKS AND ONLINE

It's a good idea to invest in a college guidebook or, if you're short on cash, check one out at your high school guidance office or the local library. These references are updated annually and have tons of detailed information about thousands of universities, as well as student perspectives or ratings on each school. But there are also some great websites that offer the same thing for free, some by the same companies that publish the books. (Be wary of anyone charging a fee for basic search info—you shouldn't have to pay.) At Seventeen.com, you can tap into *The Princeton Review*'s database, look up colleges by all sorts of different criteria, and save schools you like to your personal short list. Check out the list of additional websites and college guides in the back of this book (see page 138).

Once you've got a running list of favorite schools, start visiting their official websites. Most school sites have an admissions section, and many feature virtual tours of the campus and the opportunity to e-mail the admissions office or current students to get some of your questions answered. You can also use social networking sites like Facebook or MySpace to talk to current students, and check out campus videos on YouTube or TheU.

LOCAL COLLEGE FAIRS

Ask your guidance counselor for a schedule of local college fairs. The most well-known ones are hosted by the

17 TIP

Parents don't feel like shelling out for a cross-country college trip? Suggest you make it your family vacation this summer. Look up stuff to do nearby each school that everyone will be into, like amusement parks, beaches, sports stadiums, and museums.

National Association for College Admission Counseling (NACAC), where admissions officers from all over the world come to speak about their campuses and academic programs. This is a great chance to meet reps from schools that might be too far away to visit. For information on fairs near you, visit the NACAC website (www.nacacnet.org).

REGIONAL & HIGH SCHOOL VISITS BY ADMISSIONS REPS

Many schools send admissions officers to different cities to visit high schools and lead information sessions. Check with your guidance counselor to see which schools are scheduled to visit.

CAMPUS VISITS & OVERNIGHTS

The most expensive—but also most effective—way to get an impression of a school is to actually go there in person. Take a campus tour, sit in on an admissions information session, and schedule an overnight visit in a current student's dorm room. You'll get a firsthand look at campus life, and you can ask students, professors, and admissions officers any questions you may have.

You should definitely visit any nearby colleges that you're interested in. But for

campuses farther away you'll need to do some advance planning. Your high school may organize a college tour over spring break or summer vacation, so be sure to ask your guidance counselor about that possibility. Some colleges offer summer programs for high school students; consider enrolling in one at your favorite school and then visiting other colleges in the area during your free time.

17 MUST-ASK QUESTIONS!

Make photocopies of this worksheet for each school you're interested in and fill it out as you go on campus visits or do online research. Comparing your answers for each college will help you narrow down your options.

Name of School: _____

1 How many students attend this school?
_____
_____
_____

2 What is the tuition cost per year? Room and board cost?
_____
_____
_____

3 What kinds of scholarships are available?
_____
_____
_____

4 What are the average GPA and SAT/ACT scores of the freshman class?
_____
_____
_____

5 What are the criteria for admission?
_____
_____
_____

6 Does the school offer early admission? What are the application deadlines?
_____
_____
_____

7 What are the school's academic strengths? Does it offer my major?
_____
_____
_____

8 What is the average class size and teacher/student ratio? How accessible are the professors? What percentage of classes are taught by TAs and grad students?
_____
_____
_____

9 Is campus housing guaranteed all four years? What percentage of students live on campus?

_____
_____
_____

10 What kinds of special programs or opportunities set this school apart?

_____
_____
_____

11 What division of athletics and kinds of intramural sports are available?

_____
_____
_____

12 How diverse is the school?

_____
_____
_____

13 Is there a Greek system? How large of a role does it play in the campus social scene?

_____
_____
_____

14 What kinds of internships, research, and study-abroad opportunities are available?

_____
_____
_____

15 What percentage of students graduate in four years?

_____
_____
_____

16 What is the graduate school acceptance rate?

_____
_____
_____

17 How many applications does the school typically receive in a year, and what is the acceptance rate?

_____
_____
_____

keep track of your research

Use **The List**, below, to organize your research and thoughts about each college that you're into. As you get more information, you can take schools off the list or adjust the rankings to reflect your top picks. Remember: Your college search is a work in progress. A place that you absolutely loved in seventh grade may not make your top ten once you find out what going to school there is really like.

the list This chart will help you rank and keep track of all your favorite schools. It's a good idea to eventually focus on ten to fifteen different colleges, although you might start out by researching as many as twenty-five or thirty. Just keep in mind that the more schools you have on your list, the more research you'll have to do.

SCHOOL	CURRENT RANK	CAMPUS VISIT	WEBSITE/ BROCHURE	SAFETY/DREAM/ COMPETITIVE	STILL INTERESTED?	REASONS
example: University of Southern California	1	✓	✓	Competitive	Y	love film studies program and football games
example: University of Washington	—		✓		N	too close to home
1.						
2.						
3.						

SCHOOL	CURRENT RANK	CAMPUS VISIT	WEBSITE/ BROCHURE	SAFETY/DREAM/ COMPETITIVE	STILL INTERESTED?	REASONS
4.						
5.						
6.						
7.						
8.						
9.						
10.						
11.						
12.						
13.						
14.						
15.						

college research time line

● **7TH GRADE TO SOPHOMORE YEAR**

☐ **Start your search.** Bookmark websites of the colleges you like and be sure to check out each school's admissions page to get a heads-up on classes you may need to take in order to meet the requirements for applying.

● **JUNIOR YEAR**

☐ **Buy a college guidebook.** Now's the time to really get serious about researching schools. With a book (rather than a website), you can make notes in the margins and carry it with you to read a little before class, at lunch, or wherever.

☐ **Find out which schools offer the best programs within your field of interest.** Talk to teachers, parents, and friends about what programs or careers might go along with your interests. Decide whether a specialty school or an art, trade, or vocational program might best serve your goals.

☐ **Compile a short list.** Use **The List** (pages 44-45) to keep track of colleges that you're most interested in.

☐ **Plan some visits.** Try to make it to all the top colleges on your list to get a better sense of whether they're really right for you.

● **SENIOR YEAR**

☐ **Meet with admissions representatives.** Attend local college fairs or information sessions at your high school to get some face time with reps who can answer your last-minute questions.

☐ **Finalize your list!** Narrow down your choices and meet with your guidance counselor to go over the schools to which you want to apply.

Knowing yourself is the first step in figuring out if and where you want to go to college; getting there all begins with a little thing called the GPA. **Your high school transcript is the single most important part of your college applications**, and it all comes down to how much effort you put into class. If you take the time to do your homework, study for tests, and take challenging classes, you'll have a lot more **options**, not only for the range of colleges you can get into, but also for scholarship opportunities.

If you're a junior or senior in high school right now with a not-so-stellar GPA, you're probably thinking, "Great. Too late now." But it's not hopeless. If you have even one more semester you can spend bringing up your grades, that'll **make a good impression.** If not, keep in mind that a lot more than just grades goes into evaluating a student's transcript.

how admissions officers look at transcripts

How well you did in high school is considered a pretty good sign of how well you'll do in college. Since admissions officers know how challenging their schools' academics are, they want to know that you'll succeed and that you won't be frustrated or drop out. You don't want to be in a situation where you feel in over your head, and colleges don't want that either.

IT'S ALL ABOUT CONTEXT

Admissions officers do more than just look at your raw GPA; they also try to put that number in context. They consider the reputation of the school you attend (public, magnet, private, parochial, homeschool, community college) and the difficulty level of your classes (standard, honors, advanced placement (AP), international baccalaureate (IB), college prep). For example, if the most challenging classes offered at your school are AP, then admission officers will be looking at whether or not you have AP classes on your transcript. Admissions officers do their homework in order to understand what your achievements mean within your school environment.

GRADES VERSUS CHALLENGING COURSES

Is it better to get an A in a regular course or a B in an advanced course?
The answer, of course—which no one wants to hear—is that it's best to get an A in an advanced course! But the real issue is motivation. Are you choosing classes that guarantee you a certain GPA or are you taking ones that will stretch your mind and challenge you?

Selective colleges want to see that you're making the most of the opportunities at your fingertips. That means taking some tougher courses, such as honors, advanced placement, and international baccalaureate classes. But don't worry if your school doesn't offer any of these; admissions officers take into account what's actually available at your particular high school.

If you find that you're overwhelmed by too many advanced courses and your grades are suffering across the board, focus on just taking the advanced classes in the subjects you care most about and that you plan to continue studying in college. If you say in your application that you're a huge history buff and plan to major in it, an admissions officer would expect you to have taken the most advanced classes available in it, like AP Government or honors US History—but won't necessarily hold it against you if you take regular math classes. Whatever classes you take, you should focus on getting the best grades you can. They count for a lot because a good overall GPA proves that you're capable of doing well over the course of three or four years.

 myth It's most important to get As.

truth It's more important to challenge yourself and get the best grades possible.

17 TIP

Usually, high school counselors include a one-page overview of your high school along with their recommendations. This profile outlines the types of classes offered at the school, the average test scores of previous classes, and a list of colleges and universities attended by past graduates. This information helps an admissions committee understand your achievements in comparison to those of other students at your high school.

myth Colleges don't really count grades from freshman and sophomore years.

truth All four years of high school count!

Sure, admissions officers are going to look more closely at how you do junior and senior years, since those grades are more recent, and often the classes you take those years are harder. But your entire transcript still matters, so that means you need to work hard from freshman year on.

That said, if you totally slacked off the first two years of high school, there's still a chance to turn things around. Colleges know that some students don't get their acts together until later. If you're one of them, be prepared for the question admissions officers will be thinking: *"What happened in this person's life to cause the shift in grades?"* You don't want to just ignore it and hope they won't notice—instead, a counselor or teacher should address it in their recommendation letter. It's better to let someone else speak on your behalf, since if you do it, it could come off like you're making excuses. But as a last resort, you could include a one-paragraph statement explaining your situation and the circumstances surrounding your lower grades. This shouldn't take the place of any essay or short-answer question on the application—it should be additional. And you should only do it if you feel that your counselor or teachers *won't* properly explain it in their recommendations, which sometimes happens in schools where they rely on form letters or where there are so many students that they haven't gotten to know you personally.

planning your class schedule

Depending upon what type of college you want to attend, there are different recommended paths of study. Every high school has a set of requirements you must meet in order to graduate. Just doing the minimum is fine if you're planning to go to community college, but if you have your sights set on a more selective school, you'll need to do a little more. Plan your classes around the college you like that has the most intense course requirements. That way you'll be sure to meet or exceed the requirements at all the other places where you apply.

freshmen & sophomores

Visit the admissions sections of the websites for the colleges you're interested in and find out the minimum number of years of English, math, science, history, and foreign language they require.

juniors & seniors

Keep working to meet the requirements of your favorite schools. Design your high school class schedule so you'll be a compelling applicant, and if you feel your transcript isn't as impressive as it could be, ramp up your schedule accordingly.

HIGH SCHOOL COURSE PLANNER

Use this form to keep track of your classes, make sure you're fulfilling requirements, and plan your future schedules.

Minimum Suggested Requirements for Most Colleges	Requirements or Recommendations for Toughest School on My List	Advanced Courses Required
4 years English	___ years English	
3 years Math	___ years Math	1 _____
3 years Science	___ years Science	
3 years Social Science	___ years Social Science	2 _____
2 years Foreign Language	___ years Foreign Language	3 _____
	___ years Art	
	___ years Computer	4 _____
	___ years _____	
	___ years _____	5 _____
	___ years _____	

SPECIALIZE!

If you're really into a certain subject or future career, one way to impress an admissions office is to demonstrate that passion with your academics. Take as many classes as you can in that area. For example, if you know you want to be premed in college, take whatever medical-related courses your high school offers, like advanced courses in biology or genetics. Or if you want to work in design, take as many art-related courses as you can while still meeting the basic college requirements.

Turn the page to see the rest of your planner!

Freshman Classes

	SEMESTER 1	SEMESTER 2
1		
2		
3		
4		
5		
6		
7		
8		

Sophomore Classes

	SEMESTER 1	SEMESTER 2
1		
2		
3		
4		
5		
6		
7		
8		

Junior Classes

	SEMESTER 1	SEMESTER 2
1		
2		
3		
4		
5		
6		
7		
8		

Senior Classes

	SEMESTER 1	SEMESTER 2
1		
2		
3		
4		
5		
6		
7		
8		

when you don't make the grade

Getting a bad grade in a class doesn't mean you're doomed. Think about what might have factored into it:

Was the grade a one-time thing, or do you think you could benefit from tutoring? Figuring out what contributed to a bad mark means you can nip it in the bud and turn things around next semester, either by getting extra help or changing your schedule.

Remember that the ultimate point of getting an education isn't grades. Most of us aren't operating on the genius level, and it's rare to find people who are good at everything. Even if you've always gotten straight As in the past, everyone's strengths and weaknesses start to show in high school, when the curriculum begins to include a wider variety of subjects. Some will come easy. Some will be a huge pain. And if you're lucky, you'll find some that you absolutely love. The point of getting an education is to be able to think for yourself, to have the tools to understand and analyze the world, and to figure out your role in it. If you can graduate from high school with a better sense of how the world works, and of your interests, talents, and abilities, then you've achieved something— no matter what your report card says.

- ● **Tough subject matter?**
- ● **Overcommitted schedule?**
- ● **Not-so-great teacher?**
- ● **Outside stress (sickness, death in the family, moving, or major break-up)?**

17 TIP

If your grades take a significant dive in the second half of your senior year, you could find yourself starting college under academic probation—or, worse yet, your acceptance could be revoked altogether! Lots of students think that once those applications are turned in, they don't have to work anymore. Unfortunately, it's not true. Admissions officers often review midyear grades before making final decisions, and most schools require you to submit your final senior year transcript after you've been admitted. So don't relax until your well-earned summer vacation.

beyond the classroom

Admissions people go crazy for students who show "intellectual curiosity"— that is, they don't just stop at the required reading. If a class sparks your interest in a particular topic, go ahead and explore it more after school. It won't *feel* like school when you're reading up on it in magazines, taking road trips, visiting museums, watching movies, or attending concerts or conventions about it.

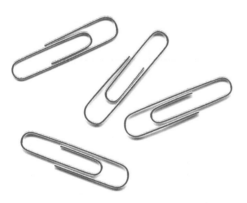

Ask your parents, teachers, librarians, bookstore employees or friends for book recommendations based on your interests. Not only will it give you something to write down for the "favorite books?" question on many applications, but it'll also improve your vocabulary, which is key for standardized tests. Your English teacher may have some summer reading lists. Amazon recommends reads based on your previous purchases or recent searches. And the Young Adult Library Services Association (YALSA) website publishes reading lists for college-bound students each year (see **Resources** on page 138). On the next page are a few favorite reading suggestions from college admission officers—but don't feel like you need to limit yourself to this list!

17 FYI

When college applications ask for a list of your outside reading, they're trying to get a sense of what ideas or subjects interest you. So unless you're interested in a career as a socialite (or, OK, a young adult fiction author), maybe don't put down *Gossip Girl #7*.

NOT YOUR TYPICAL SUMMER READING LIST

if you enjoy... Science
- *The Elegant Universe: Superstrings, Hidden Dimensions, and the Quest for the Ultimate Theory* by Brian Greene
- *Promised the Moon: The Untold Story of the First Women in the Space Race* by Stephanie Nolen
- *Stiff: The Curious Lives of Human Cadavers* by Mary Roach

if you enjoy... History
- *First They Killed My Father: A Daughter of Cambodia Remembers* by Loung Ung
- *Witch Hunt: Mysteries of the Salem Witch Trials* by Marc Aronson
- *Six Wives: The Queens of Henry VIII* by David Starkey

if you enjoy... Contemporary Literature
- *Middlesex* by Jeffrey Eugenides
- *Special Topics in Calamity Physics* by Marisha Pessl
- *In the Time of the Butterflies* by Julia Alvarez

if you enjoy... Social Science
- *Guns, Germs and Steel: The Fates of Human Societies* by Jared Diamond
- *Riding the Bus with My Sister: A True Life Journey* by Rachel Simon
- *Speak Truth to Power: Human Rights Defenders Who Are Changing Our World* by Kerry Kennedy

if you enjoy... Sports
- *Friday Night Lights: A Town, a Team, and a Dream* by H. G. Bissinger
- *Counting Coup: A True Story of Basketball and Honor on the Little Big Horn* by Larry Colton
- *On Wings of Joy: The Story of Ballet from the 16th Century to Today* by Trudy Garfunkel

if you enjoy... Fantasy
- *The Golden Compass* by Philip Pullman
- *Dune* by Frank Herbert
- *The Amulet of Samarkand* by Jonathan Stroud

academic time line

● FRESHMAN YEAR

☐ **Do your homework.** You might not get all the answers right, but just trying will earn the respect of your teachers—they'll be more willing to work with you (and maybe even negotiate your grade) if they know you've been making an effort all along.

☐ **Establish good relationships with your teachers.** Actively participate in class discussions. Ask questions. Raise your hand. At smaller schools, you might have these same teachers again in the coming years—and need them to write recommendation letters.

☐ **Practice good study habits.** Figure out a routine that works for you. Maybe doing your homework right after school is when you're most alert, or maybe you work better after dinner. You know yourself best, so listen to your body and plan your schedule accordingly.

☐ **Take electives that tie in with your interests.** Non-required classes give you a chance to explore new subjects.

☐ **Plan ahead.** Make sure you're aware of the minimum academic recommendations at your favorite colleges—if there are any classes you need four years of, sign up for them now.

☐ **Enroll in a foreign language.** Most schools require a minimum of two years, and top institutions will look for three or four. Get started now, so that by junior year you'll have more options available to you. Bonus: Learning another language—especially Latin—can boost your SAT vocabulary score, since many English words have roots in other languages.

● SOPHOMORE YEAR

☐ **Find out what advanced programs your high school offers.** Consider enrolling in advanced classes in subjects you enjoy and do well in.

☐ **Read unassigned books.** Boost your vocabulary and get "intellectual curiosity" points by reading non-required books on topics that interest you.

☐ **Meet with your assigned guidance counselor.** Take the initiative to introduce yourself to your guidance counselor and ask what resources are available to help you in your college search and application process.

☐ **If you haven't already, now's the time to enroll in a foreign language.** Look at what languages are offered at your high school and think about which one you might use most in your future career.

● JUNIOR YEAR

☐ **Focus on your grades.** If you haven't earned the greatest GPA, this is the year to get focused and turn things around.

☐ **Beef up your schedule with advanced classes.** If you're applying to top schools, you should be taking several advanced courses. Also, sign up for any AP or IB exams given this year.

☐ **Make a plan for senior year.** Double check that have taken or will take all the classes you need to be the most competitive applicant for your top schools.

● SENIOR YEAR

☐ **Keep it up!** Continue to maintain your grades, even after you turn in all of your applications.

In one of the best high school movies of all time, *Election*, the female lead, Tracy Flick, played by Reese Witherspoon, is the perfect stereotype of the overachieving student. As over-the-top as her character may seem, there are actually plenty of students out there just like her who think there's some **perfect formula** for getting into college and who'll do whatever it takes to fill their resumes with activities, leadership, and accolades. But the Tracy Flicks have got it all wrong. **There are no guarantees when it comes to college admissions**, and there's no secret checklist that every admissions officer fills out as she reads through the stacks of applications.

When admissions officers

review your extracurriculars—as with the entire application—they're trying to get a sense of who you are and how you're different from everyone else who's applying. Some of the worst applications are from those students who seem to think that colleges are just looking for people who can fill in the most blanks—because nothing sets those students apart. It's a waste of time to participate in activities only because you think it'll look good on your applications. Think about the story you want to tell to colleges and what role each of your activities and commitments play. Are you passionate about politics and social change? Then there should be fund-raising organizations or other political groups on your application—not a laundry list of every club your school offers. Are you an aspiring actress? It's okay if you list only the local theater in your activities section, as long as you describe the hours spent in rehearsals, your volunteer work teaching improv to kindergarteners there, and your role as head of the publicity committee.

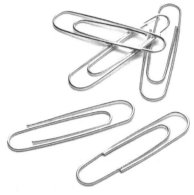

myth Colleges are looking for well-rounded students.

truth Colleges are trying to create well-rounded *campuses* populated with specialized students.

17 FYI

Just as grades show how well you might do in the college classroom, activities and leadership show how you might get involved in the campus community.

the three Cs

Three things to keep in mind as you apply to college are **commitment**, **continuity**, and **curiosity**.

COMMITMENT

One measure of a person's passion is her sense of commitment to whatever she loves. A dedicated athlete will spend hours, days, and years training to be the best she can be. Your level of commitment says a lot about what a university can expect from you during your time on campus.

CONTINUITY

It's also important to make sure there's continuity between what you enjoy studying and how you spend your time outside the classroom. College applications ask questions about what you do, what you read, how you spend your summers, and whom you admire. Each of your answers is a piece of the puzzle they're constructing to get a more complete picture of you as a person. Instead of looking at each of these as separate questions, think about how they relate to each another and see if you can weave a common theme among all your application answers.

CURIOSITY

Are you open to new ideas and experiences? Do you ask questions about how and why things work? Do you go beyond just what you have to do for class to explore your interests? Showing that you're curious about the world tells schools that you'll bring new insights, questions and ways of thinking to your department at college.

17 TIP

Think about how the books you read, the activities you do, and the things you love are related to one another. Maybe they all involve a sense of adventure, or helping people, or solving problems. They might seem totally random at first, but look closer.

IF YOU'RE INTERESTED IN...	THEN YOU SHOULD...
working with kids	■ read books at an elementary school ■ teach children's classes at your church, mosque, or temple ■ volunteer to be a Big Sister
fashion	■ work in the costume department of your school's theater ■ get a job at a local boutique ■ participate in a fashion show at your high school
journalism	■ write for your school newspaper ■ get a summer internship at your local paper ■ publish a blog
film/theater	■ try out for school or community productions ■ take a film production class at your local community college ■ work as a production assistant on films shot locally
social change	■ participate in the debate team ■ volunteer with a grass-roots organization ■ join Model United Nations
medicine	■ volunteer as a hospital candy striper ■ intern as an assistant to a medical researcher ■ take a CPR/first-aid certification course
other cultures	■ join a language or cultural club at your high school ■ spend a summer or semester abroad as an exchange student ■ work at an ethnic restaurant
politics	■ run for student body government ■ volunteer for a local campaign ■ organize an event to raise awareness about a political issue of importance to you
helping others	■ volunteer at the animal rescue shelter ■ work at a retirement home ■ tutor a grade-schooler
music	■ join your school's choir, orchestra, or singing group ■ start a band ■ work at your local radio station or music store

beyond school activities

While school clubs and sports are one measure of your involvement, admissions committees also take note of outside activities that you dedicate a big chunk of time to. As you fill out your applications, make sure you not only list what you do but also the amount of time and commitment each thing demands.

AFTER-SCHOOL JOBS

Many students hold down a job in high school for a variety of reasons: to earn extra spending money, pay for car insurance, save for college, contribute to household expenses, or gain real-world experience in a career area. Some work because they want to, others because they have to. If a job is sucking up a major percentage of your time, tell the admissions committee why—especially if the reason is a little more impressive or noble than "so I can buy a Vera Wang prom dress."

COMMUNITY SERVICE

If you enjoy making a difference in your community, find ways to volunteer that go along with your interests. You may be able to get involved at a much more significant level than you would in a school club by working on political campaigns, at a retirement home, or at your city's homeless shelter.

INTERNSHIPS

If you're inspired by a certain academic subject, look into research opportunities at the nearest university or hospital. Talk to your teachers; they may be able to point you in the right direction. If you're

17 TIP

Applications often ask you to explain your most significant area of involvement—but don't mistake *significance* for biggest time commitment. Being on the swim team may take up most of your time, but maybe playing with a garage band is your greatest passion. Answer this question honestly, and describe the activity that's the most important to you and why.

A volunteer is someone who does something without being forced to. If you're only participating in community service because it will look good on your college application, then you're pretty much missing the point—and admissions officers have a pretty good eye for spotting resume padding. At the same time if your high school or the colleges to which you're applying do require a certain number of volunteer hours, then you'll want to find something that you enjoy. One good way to get started is to take a look at social networking sites like MySpace, which features an activist search section, and Youthnoise (www.youthnoise.com), a website by and for young people that publicizes outreach opportunities at the local, national, and global levels. By connecting with other student volunteers, you should be able to find some ideas that are meaningful to you.

17 TIP

Be creative in your volunteer efforts. If you're into sports, consider working the sidelines of a local running event or coaching a girls' soccer team. Love the arts? Put on a coffeehouse night featuring artists and musicians, then donate the proceeds to your favorite charity. Focus on what you're passionate about and chances are you'll touch others' lives along the way.

interested in scientific research, apply to be a lab assistant. If you love art history, work at a local museum or auction house. You might start out washing test tubes or making photocopies, but you'll gain great exposure to a field and show how committed you are.

RELIGIOUS AFFILIATION

Spiritual commitments can play a significant role in a person's life. Depending on your faith and how invested you are in it, it might require a lot of your time. Since religious and cultural groups are a big part of any university campus, you might want to highlight how your faith has had an impact on your high school experience and how you plan to continue your commitment during college—maybe by participating in interfaith campus groups or pursuing a degree in religious studies.

SPECIAL TALENTS

You may not have time to get involved in the debate team or Spanish club at your high school if you're busy launching a semi-professional career as a dancer or a nationally lauded violinist. If you have a special talent or ability that can't quite be captured on a traditional application, feel free to include audio-visual aids: a DVD showing your performances, a CD of your music, or a portfolio of your artwork. When your activities go above and beyond the traditional expectations, colleges note that type of commitment and it counts for a lot.

SPORTS

If you're a competitive athlete hoping to participate in college sports, you may be on outside teams in addition to your high school one. Or you may be involved in a sport that's not offered at your high school, like snowboarding, gymnastics, equestrianism, wakeboarding, sailing, rock climbing, motocross, surfing, or ice-skating. Colleges usually begin recruiting high school athletes in their junior year, so keep a file of your athletic accomplishments in your **activities folder**. Write down any leadership positions (like captain) and when you held them, significant competitions, records broken, awards you've won, and the hours you devote each week to your sport. Also begin compiling footage for a supplemental video if you're hoping to get recruited for college teams.

SUMMER ADVENTURES

Colleges love hearing how you spent your time off, so don't just hang out all vacation. Take a cooking class, travel, get an internship, or do a theater program. Just make sure you have something interesting to talk about when an interviewer wants to know what you did last summer.

myth You must complete a minimum number of volunteer hours to get into college.

truth Most colleges don't have a volunteerism requirement for admission.

17 TIP

If there's something you love to do that's not offered at your school, either get involved outside of school or start a new club! (The first step is usually to find a teacher willing to be your club advisor; your principal or vice principal can tell you how to go from there.) The earlier in high school you start participating in an activity, the better your chances of demonstrating commitment over the course of several years.

BRAG SHEET

Keep track of your activities, hours of commitment each week, leadership positions held, and why each activity is meaningful to you. If you don't have enough space, make a copy of this sheet and keep it in your **activities folder**.

ACTIVITY	LEADERSHIP POSITION	YEARS INVOLVED	HOURS EACH WEEK	WHY IS THIS ACTIVITY MEANINGFUL TO ME?
1				
2				
3				
4				
5				
6				
7				
8				
9				
10				

how to become a leader

1. IDENTIFY AN AREA WHERE YOU CAN MAKE A DIFFERENCE

Start by doing what you know and what you're best at. Join clubs and activities that sound like they're up your alley. You'll probably have to start at the bottom, and it may be frustrating at first when you're asked to do things like stuff envelopes or make photocopies. But remember: Everyone has to start somewhere. And if you have a positive attitude and work hard, people will start to give you more responsibility and ask for your input.

17 FYI

Don't freak out if you've moved and have to start all over getting involved in organizations at your new school. Admissions officers recognize the challenges transfer students face and take that into consideration.

17 TIP

Think about how you can improve things in your school and community. How can you make the world—or at least your corner of it—a better place? If you're running for a leadership office, what will you accomplish in that position? If you write for the school paper, how can you make it better? If you're involved in theater, what kinds of messages do you want to share with your community?

2. HAVE A VISION

When you have a clear sense of where you want to go and how you're going to get there, you'll inspire confidence in other people and they'll naturally want to follow your lead. So think about what you want to accomplish. Is your goal to increase your school's newspaper circulation? Implement a recycling program? Get a great band to play at Homecoming? When you and your friends are putting in long hours on the yearbook staff or working weekends at a carwash fund-raiser, there'll be times when you have to remind them (and yourself) of the vision in order to stay motivated. So write down your goals and keep them in mind as you go to work.

3. BE WILLING TO TAKE RISKS

Taking risks is scary because it opens up the possibility for failure. What if you run for office and lose? What if you decide to try a new play as captain of the soccer team, and it results in the other team scoring and winning the game? Whenever you try anything, there's always the possibility that you'll disappoint yourself or others. But if you never have the courage to take a leap of faith, you'll never know what you're capable of achieving.

4. DELEGATE AND MOTIVATE

When you try to do everything yourself, you're not actually *leading* anyone. You're also likely to suffer from stress and burnout and have trouble reaching your goals. Learn to ask for help and trust the other people in your group to do a good job.

People love to be recognized for what they do well. If you're organizing a fund-raiser at your school, think about who's great at marketing and advertising, or organizing logistics, or sweet-talking the principal to get permission. Give people responsibilities that match their talents, and let them know that's why you're giving them those assignments—because you know you can count on them.

17 FYI

As admissions officers read through thousands of applications, the ones that rise to the top are those with a vision—a sense of what you want to experience in college, what you're going to bring to a classroom, how you're going to be involved in campus life, and what kind of impact you're going to leave after you graduate.

5. REWARD YOURSELF AND OTHERS

Learn to celebrate the little and big victories you achieve, and enjoy the journey as much as the finish. Also be sure to show your appreciation to everyone who helped you reach your goals. Plan a wrap party. Take your team out for ice cream. Publicly thank everyone who played a part in your success. People love to be acknowledged, and chances are if you value your team they'll want to work with you again.

four-year planner

Add your favorite suggestions from this chapter to the **Master Calendar** at the front of the book (see page 6).

● FRESHMAN YEAR

☐ **Try out a variety of activities.** Sit in on different club meetings to get a sense of which you might enjoy. Think about how you like to spend your free time and see if there's an activity or group that matches your interests.

● SOPHOMORE YEAR

☐ **Start thinking about running for an office in one of your clubs or organizations.** If there's something you enjoy doing and no club for it, start one! Admissions officers love initiative.

● JUNIOR YEAR

☐ **This is your time to shine.** Step up and be a leader. Even if you don't hold an official leadership position, offer to head up a special project. Focus your time and energy on the extracurricular activities that are the most important to you and ditch the ones you've lost interest in or that are taking you away from doing things you love more.

● SENIOR YEAR

☐ **Make your last year count.** If you haven't gotten involved in anything yet, now is the time to add meaningful activities to your schedule. Figure out the one or two interests you're going to focus on in your college applications and join clubs, organizations, or groups that match them. Don't aimlessly try to fill a resume with whatever opportunities are available. Remember, colleges aren't necessarily looking for well-rounded students. Stick with your passions and highlight your unique commitments.

In addition to your grades and your activities, colleges also want to know **how you think and what you have to say**. Enter the college essay. It lets you talk directly to admissions officers in your own voice and show off your personality and creativity, which might not be fully captured in the rest of the application. This is your **chance to speak your mind**; often sthere aren't even any guidelines—you can write about whatever you want. An amazing essay can be the thing that pushes an okay application into the acceptance pile, so take some time to think about what you're going to say and how you want to say it.

write what you know

How many times have we all heard that? Still, it's especially true with your college essay, where you have only 500 words or less to impress an admissions reader. Use your answers from the **Character Sketch** (see page 21) to start brainstorming ideas for your essays. This is a great way to get in touch with the experiences, events, and moments in your life that have helped define who you are. On a blank sheet of paper, write down any and all of these that come to mind.

BE ORIGINAL AND PERSONAL

Now take a look at your brainstorm and circle the thoughts or experiences that best express who you are and what's important to you. Do you see any themes developing? What ideas or interests set you apart from your family, your peers, or other people in your community? Maybe it's your obsession with a certain band or your need to start every day with ten minutes of meditation or your knack for finding an alternative use for everyday household items or the role you play within your circle of friends. When you use them as jumping-off points for painting a picture of who you are, any of these would make a great essay topic.

top ten college essay topics to avoid

Here are a few topics that are guaranteed to put an admissions officer to sleep. It's not that these experiences aren't valid or important. It's just that they either don't help you look like a great candidate or they're way overused and all start to sound alike. The point of the college essay is to stand out, so you don't want to follow the crowd—but you don't want to stand out for all the wrong reasons, either. So unless a college specifically asks you to write about one of these topics, it's safer to avoid them.

1 **The time you built houses in Mexico with your youth group or visited Israel to explore your cultural heritage**—While these are both wonderful ways to spend your vacation, volunteering or traveling abroad with a school or youth group has become a really common high school experience and the subject of many a college essay. It's better to mention these elsewhere in the application than to risk sounding the same as everybody else.

2 **Your parents' divorce**—There are three reasons to avoid the divorce topic: It's (unfortunately) common, it's not necessarily about *you*, and it's hard to do it justice in the small space provided.

3 **Coming to America**—Again, while being an immigrant is an important experience, it also frequently appears in college essays. And many students who were really little or not even born yet when their families came over make the mistake of writing about their parents' or grandparents' journey. It may be a great story, but it doesn't really tell much about the girl herself.

4 **Why your grades are so low or why you weren't involved in extracurricular activities**—Bottom line, the essay is *not* the right place to make excuses; if necessary, include a separate paragraph explaining your grades or use the activity space on the application to explain your lack of involvement. On the other hand, some extenuating circumstances that shed light on who you are, like battling a sickness, getting in a car accident, or helping your single parent raise your siblings can be great essay topics if well-written.

5 **A narrative version of your resume**—It's fine to go into greater detail or tell a story about something you've already mentioned, but don't use the valuable essay space just to repeat info you have already included in your application.

6 **The death of a relative**—There's no denying the dramatic impact that the loss of a loved one can have on you; it's something that affects us all. But because of that, it is a common essay topic. And the more distant the relative, the more it might look like an insincere attempt to drum up sympathy.

7 **Why a particular college is so great**—Colleges know all about what makes them great, but they don't know what it is that makes you so fabulous. Some students make the mistake of writing a mini-research paper on the school instead of talking about themselves. If the application specifically asks why you want to go to the school either as an essay or short answer question, make sure you talk about who you are and why the school is a good fit for you.

8 **Other people's experiences**—Don't sell yourself short by telling someone else's story. You're just as interesting as anybody else! Keep it personal and memorable.

9 **Topics that are just too big for 500 words,** like your stand on abortion or the death penalty. You risk confusing the reader and not getting your point across when you try to tackle a subject better suited for a research paper.

10 **Another school's essay topic**—Don't reuse a writing sample that doesn't completely fit the essay question. Students who applied to University of Chicago a few years ago were asked to write about a jar of mustard, so any other college that received an essay mentioning mustard knew that student had just cut and pasted their essay. Colleges want to feel special and know that you're really excited about the prospect of attending their schools, and that means taking the time to fill out their applications.

17 TIP

If you do use one essay for all your college applications, make sure you carefully proofread each one, so that you don't accidentally mention names, places, or programs that don't apply to every school. Your essay about cheerleading that ends with the hope of cheering for the Ohio State Buckeyes probably won't go over too well at the University of Michigan or Florida State.

tell a story

As you brainstorm essay topics, keep in mind that you're telling a story, albeit a brief one. What makes for a good story? Compelling characters and an interesting situation, often with an interesting complication and resolution. Be careful if your writing has a tendency to be mysterious or hard to decode—it might reflect your personality, but you still want the reader to get your point. Know exactly what that point is and be sure you've made it clear by the end of the essay. If you think of the whole application as a puzzle, the essay is the missing piece that completes the picture of who you are. This is the place to get across the parts of your character that aren't covered anywhere else, or to go even deeper into an aspect of yourself that's important but only briefly mentioned in another section of the application.

be authentic

One of the biggest essay mistakes is trying to be someone you're not. Don't be funny if comedy isn't your strong suit, and don't conjure up a sob story because you think you'll earn points by tugging on the admissions committee's heartstrings. They read a lot of essays, and they can spot the ones that are trying too hard from a mile away. The real you is much more refreshing. In an authentic story, the student's personality jumps off the page— and that's not easily forgotten.

17 TIP

Don't wait until the last minute to write your essay. Give yourself more time than you think you need to come up with original ideas, get feedback from family or teachers, and fine-tune your masterpiece.

add detail

It's the details that set you apart, and the more specific you are, the less you'll sound like everybody else. Be descriptive. Say something new instead of repeating the same thought a different way. You want the reader to hear, see, touch, and feel your experiences.

Typical Essay Prompts

On a separate sheet of paper, try your hand at a few of these sample topics to get some practice mastering the five-hundred-word essay.

1 Describe an event or experience in your life that shaped who you are today.

2 Submit page 231 of your five-hundred-page biography.

3 Describe one of the biggest challenges you have had to overcome.

4 Discuss an issue that concerns you in the world at large or right at your doorstep.

proofread

Before you send off your essay,

make sure you reread it and recruit your teachers, friends, and family to do the same. Find someone you trust to proofread it for grammatical, spelling, and punctuation errors. Also, consider asking a person who knows you—but not as well as your family or best friends—to read your essay. Maybe a teacher, mentor, or college student. Ask them whether or not after reading the essay they have a better sense of who you are or if there's anything that seems unclear or out of place. Oftentimes people you're close with will read between the lines and use what they already know about you to understand a passage that wouldn't make sense to a stranger.

Remember that writing is a personal process, and while there are some general dos and don'ts, there's no formula for creating the perfect college essay. It has to come from the heart. The more you're able to find and trust your own voice, the more memorable and effective your essay will be.

17 TIP

Avoid using clichés in your essays. While it may be easier to rely on catchphrases like "following my heart" or "counting my blessings" admissions officers want to hear your voice, and when you only have five hundred words, every one counts!

How much do you love standardized testing?! Yeah, we're with you. Even though it's pretty much known that **test scores** aren't necessarily great for predicting a student's talent or potential, they are still required at most universities. Luckily, if you're one of the many people who think they're terrible test-takers, there are **tons of resources** out there to help you **improve your score**.

17 FYI

Instead of just looking at your overall scores, many schools will separate out the sections and take your highest reading, highest math, and highest writing scores. So taking the SAT more than once can work to your

advantage because you might be able to improve one of your *individual* scores, even if your overall score stays the same. And sometimes just being more familiar with the test format the second time around can boost your numbers.

17 TIP

If you want to get a head start prepping for the PSAT/NMSQT, sign up to take it during your sophomore year for practice. OK, practicing for the practice test sounds a little crazy! But it might help you do better on your junior year PSAT, when your score counts for scholarship consideration.

myth If I don't have high test scores, I can't get into college.

truth Test scores are only one of many factors a college considers when selecting students, and some schools don't even require them. Don't let low numbers get you down; play up your strengths in your applications and rest assured that there are great colleges out there looking for students with just your qualifications.

types of tests

There are two main types of standardized testing accepted by colleges and universities: the ACT and the SAT. The PLAN and PSAT/NMSQT are practice tests for the real deal. Testing schedules and registration are available online (see **resources**, page 138).

The ACT (originally known as the American College Testing program) is a set of four multiple-choice tests (five, if you take the optional writing test), and it covers English, math, reading, and science.

The SAT (or Scholastic Assessment Test) has three main sections: critical reading, math, and writing. The critical reading section has multiple-choice questions that test you on sentence completions and reading comprehension. The math section tests you on numbers and operations; algebra and functions; geometry and measurement; and data, statistics, and probability. The writing section includes multiple-choice questions dealing with improving sentences and paragraphs, and an essay.

There are also SAT Subject Tests, which focus on more specific subject areas. Tests are offered throughout the year in literature, history, science, and languages.

Some schools require that applicants submit a few SAT Subject Test scores, and often homeschooled students are asked to take multiple subject tests as an another way of measuring what they've learned over the last four years. Check with the admissions office at each school to which you're applying to find out if subject tests are required or recommended.

If you're in advanced placement (AP) or international baccalaureate (IB) classes, you'll have the chance to take additional tests in those subjects. Unlike the more general SAT and ACT, the AP and IB tests are designed to get at knowledge you acquired during those specific courses. And while most colleges don't require that you take these tests or even report your scores, if you do well (AP score of 3 or above; IB score of 4 or above) submitting them will not only help you get into college, it may also get you advanced standing or college credit.

choosing your tests

Fall of sophomore year is when you'd usually take the PLAN (the practice test for the ACT), and fall of junior year is when you'll need to take the PSAT/NMSQT (Preliminary SAT/National Merit Scholarship Qualifying Test). Once you get the results, you'll have an idea of your testing strengths and weaknesses, and you'll also see how you stack up against other college-bound students. If you take both tests, you'll also know which one you're better at, so you can take the final version of just that one. Another reason to take the practice test: Your PSAT/NMSQT score from junior year can put you in the running for National Merit Scholarships.

Take the SAT or ACT in the spring of junior year. This gives you enough time to take another one in early summer or fall of senior year if you want to try and improve your scores. If you're really not happy with your SAT scores, you may want to try taking the ACT—or vice versa. Most schools requiring standardized tests will accept either one; just be sure to double-check with the admissions offices.

After checking which of your colleges require SAT Subjects Tests, decide which ones to take based on that *and* on your class schedule. You'll want to be tested on material that's fresh in your mind, so go with the subjects that you're best at and that you'll be studying in the spring of junior year and the fall of senior year.

TEST TRACKER

Keep track of all your SAT, ACT, AP/IB, and subject tests, and don't forget to add the dates to your master calendar!

TEST	DATE	SCORES

general testing strategies

It's a good idea to do some prep work beforehand, whether it's taking a practice test online, reading through a test prep book, or attending a class. Knowing what kind of material will be on the test and the different types of questions you'll see will help you feel more comfortable on test day and almost automatically earn you a few extra points. Here are some general testing strategies to keep in mind as you get ready.

- Understand the directions for each section before test day so that you can use those extra minutes for answering questions.

- If you don't know the answer but can rule out one or two of the choices, try making an educated guess.

- Skip questions that are taking up too much time or that you know you can't answer—giving a wrong answer hurts your score more than not answering at all. Just be sure to mark the questions you didn't answer, and if you have more time at the end of the test, go back to them.

- Answer sentence completions first since they take less time than the reading comprehension questions.

- If a vocabulary word has you stumped, think about how the root, prefix, or suffix is similar to other words you do know, and then make an educated guess about its meaning.

- Double-check your answer sheet to make sure that your answers correctly correspond to the question numbers.

- Your essay should include an introduction plus one or two well-developed points that support your argument.

when your scores don't add up

Check out the average scores of admitted students at the schools to which you're applying. If yours are way off the mark, you may need to rethink things a bit and apply to a few extra schools where you fall within the median or where standardized testing isn't required. While it's still an important part of the college application process at most schools, there are a growing number that either don't require it or give you the option of submitting alternatives, such as additional writing samples or a high GPA. For a listing of colleges that offer these alternatives, visit www.fairtest.org.

101 words to know before test day

These are some of the most common vocab words to show up on standardized tests. Cut out the flashcards, store them in the pocket folder, and use them to quiz yourself before the big day!

17 TIP

Studying up on your vocab will help you eliminate incorrect answers and give you a better understanding of the reading passages.

ABSOLVE (V.)	**ACRIMONY** (N.)
AFFECTATION (N.)	**ALACRITY** (N.)
AMALGAMATION (N.)	**ANACHRONISTIC** (ADJ.)
ASSIDUOUS (ADJ.)	**AUDACIOUS** (ADJ.)
BANE (N.)	**BERATE** (V.)
BILK (V.)	**BOON** (N. OR ADJ.)

bitterness or harshness of manner or speech, animosity	to forgive, free from guilt or duty
eager willingness, often with quick lively action	a pretending to like; artificial behavior
out of its proper historical time	a uniting or combination of smaller parts
bold, daring, insolent	diligent, persevering, careful
to scold severely	cause of harm or ruin; source of annoyance
a welcome benefit, blessing; merry	to cheat or swindle, defraud

CACOPHONY (N.)	**CALUMNY** (N.)
CLOYING (ADJ.)	**COLLUSION** (N.)
CONUNDRUM (N.)	**CULPABLE** (ADJ.)
DEBACLE (N.)	**DELETERIOUS** (ADJ.)
DESPOTISM (N.)	**DILATORY** (ADJ.)
DOGMATIC (ADJ.)	**EFFICACIOUS** (ADJ.)

a false and malicious statement, slander	harsh, jarring sound; discord
a secret agreement for fraudulent or illegal activity; conspiracy	overly sweet or rich
deserving blame	a riddle or puzzling problem
harmful to health; injurious	a crushing defeat or ruinous collapse
causing delay; slow, tardy	dominance by an absolute ruler or tyrant
effective	asserted without proof; stating opinion positively or arrogantly

EMEND (V.)	**ENDEMIC** (ADJ.)
EXPURGATE (V.)	**FELICITOUS** (ADJ.)
FERAL (ADJ.)	**FORGE** (N. OR V.)
FORTITUDE (N.)	**GOAD** (V.)
GOURMAND (N.)	**HACKNEYED** (ADJ.)
HARANGUE (N. OR V.)	**IMPUGN** (V.)

prevalent in a particular locality, as a disease or plant	to correct a text
expressed in a way suitable to the occasion; appropriate	to remove what is considered obscene; censor
to move forward steadily; to imitate fraudulently, to counterfeit; to form or shape; a place where metal is wrought	untamed, wild, savage
to prod or urge	patient endurance of trouble or pain; courage
clichéd, made trite by overuse	one who loves good food and drink and indulges excessively
to oppose or challenge as false	a long ranting speech, tirade; to address with a long ranting speech

IMPUTE (V.)	**INEFFABLE** (ADJ.)
INSIDIOUS (ADJ.)	**IRRESOLUTE** (ADJ.)
JOLLITY (N.)	**JUXTAPOSITION** (N.)
LARCENY (N.)	**LATENT** (ADJ.)
LOATH (ADJ.)	**LUMMOX** (N.)
MAVERICK (N.)	**MAXIM** (N.)

inexpressible, too sacred to be spoken	to attribute (esp. a fault or misconduct) to another
wavering, indecisive	characterized by treachery or slyness, more dangerous than seems evident
side-by-side placement	cheerfulness, liveliness, merriness
hidden and undeveloped in a person or thing	theft of property
a clumsy or stupid person	reluctant
a concise rule of conduct	an unbranded animal; one who takes an independent stand

MISSIVE (N.)	MORASS (N.)
NEGLIGIBLE (ADJ.)	NONDESCRIPT (ADJ.)
NOVICE (N.)	OBSTINATE (ADJ.)
OBSTREPEROUS (ADJ.)	OPULENCE (N.)
OSTENSIBLE (ADJ.)	OSTRACISM (N.)
PARAMOUNT (ADJ.)	PERFIDIOUS (ADJ.)

marsh, an area of soggy ground; a confusing or messy situation	a letter or written message
hard to classify or describe	so small or unimportant that it can be disregarded, trifling
determined to have one's own way, stubborn	a person new to something, beginner
lavish wealth or abundance	noisy or unruly, esp. in resisting
exclusion or banishment	apparent
disloyal or untrustworthy	ranking higher than any other, chief

PERFUNCTORY (ADJ.)	PERSPICACIOUS (ADJ.)
POTENTATE (N.)	PROMULGATE (V.)
PROSAIC (ADJ.)	PUNDIT (N.)
QUANDARY (N.)	QUERULOUS (ADJ.)
QUIP (N. OR V.)	RAZE (V.)
REBUFF (N. OR V.)	REMISS (ADJ.)

having keen judgment, discerning	done in a routine manner, superficial, indifferent
to make known officially, to make widespread	a person having great power, ruler or monarch
a person of great learning	commonplace, dull
inclined to find fault, complaining	a state of uncertainty, dilemma
to tear down, demolish	a witty or sarcastic remark; to make a witty or sarcastic remark
careless, negligent	an abrupt refusal of advice or help; to snub

REPUDIATE (V.)	**SACROSANCT** (ADJ.)
SHUN (V.)	**SPECIOUS** (ADJ.)
SUBTERFUGE (N.)	**SURREPTITIOUS** (ADJ.)
SYCOPHANT (N.)	**TANGENTIAL** (ADJ.)
TEMERITY (N.)	**TIMOROUS** (ADJ.)
TORPID (ADJ.)	**TRACTABLE** (ADJ.)

very sacred or holy	to reject, refuse to have anything to do with
seeming to be good or correct without really being so	to keep away from, avoid deliberately
done in a stealthy way	any plan or action used to hide or evade
digressing; not relating to the main point	one who seeks favor by flattering people of wealth or influence
full of fear, timid, afraid	foolish or rash boldness
easily managed, docile	dull, sluggish, dormant

TREMULOUS (ADJ.)	**UNFETTER** (V.)
USURP (V.)	**UTILITARIAN** (ADJ.)
VACILLATE (V.)	**VARIEGATED** (ADJ.)
VENERATE (V.)	**VERDANT** (ADJ.)
VERISIMILITUDE (N.)	**VIRULENT** (ADJ.)
VITIATED (ADJ.)	**WANE** (V.)

to free from restraint	trembling, quivering, fearful, timid
something useful, stressing usefulness over beauty	to take by force
having variety, marked with different colors or spots	to waver, fluctuate, show indecision
green, covered with vegetation	to deeply respect, or revere
extremely poisonous, deadly; highly infectious; bitterly antagonistic or hateful	the appearance of being true or real
to grow dim, to decline in power	spoiled, corrupted, invalidated

WHEEDLE
(V.)

WILY
(ADJ.)

YAMMER
(V.)

ZEALOUS
(ADJ.)

ZEPHYR
(N.)

fill in these blank flash cards with any other vocab words

crafty, sly	to influence or get by flattery
of or showing zeal, fervent	to whine, whimper or complain
	a gentle breeze; something airy or unsubstantial

B eyond your grades, activities, leadership, essay, and test scores, there's one more thing that, at many schools, plays a big role in the **admissions process: what other people think of you**. Anyone can look good on paper, but colleges want to make sure you really are as great as you seem. That's where recommendation letters and personal interviews come in.

the power of publicity

Recommendations and interviews are a chance for the admissions committee to see you through the eyes of someone else— someone who can give a second opinion on your personality and achievements and who can help predict what kind of college student you'll be. A teacher writing a rec letter might say whether or not you participate in class discussions, do your work on time, show real potential in a certain subject, or go beyond just what's expected of you. A guidance counselor might say how you've grown as a student throughout high school or how you've influenced the school during your time there.

The point of the college application is to sell yourself to the admissions committee. You'll spend lots of time talking about your accomplishments and aspirations, and while all that bragging is necessary to convince the college that you belong there, your recommendation letters are also necessary to back up what you've said and maybe even add something you forgot to say or didn't think was worth mentioning. It's one thing to say how, as editor-in-chief of your school newspaper, you challenged your staff to write compelling stories, expanded the editorial section, and increased readership. But it's even more powerful when someone else says it.

deciding who to ask

To get the best recommendation letters, choose teachers who know you well so that they can personalize their letters as much as possible. Start being friendly with the teachers you like most—drop by their desks after class to ask a question or make a comment, and work up to mentioning your future plans and the schools you're considering. It'll give them a chance to get to know you, and you might even get some useful advice.

Make sure to get at least one recommendation from a teacher in an academic subject—rather than, say, music or gym. Colleges want to hear from people who've taught you in the main subjects like English, math, science, or history. You may have two P.E. teachers who know you really, really well and will write great personal letters, but the admissions office is going to wonder why you didn't get a recommendation from an academic teacher...like, is it because none of them would say anything good?

It's also a good idea to pick teachers in subjects that match up with your interests. If it's clear from your application that you want to study medicine, it's great to have a recommendation from a science teacher who can talk about your enthusiasm and talent in chemistry or biology. If you're into journalism, it would make sense to have a recommendation from either an English teacher or the newspaper or literary magazine adviser.

Some schools require additional recommendations from peers, religious leaders (if you're applying to a religiously affiliated school), employers, coaches, or community members. As you would with your teacher recommendations, choose people who know about the aspects of your personality that you plan to highlight in your applications.

requesting recommendation letters

- Get your recommendation forms by early fall of your senior year so that you can give people at least a month to write them.

- Make photocopies of the **Recommendation Info Sheet** on page 102 and give it to each recommender along with a copy of your most recent transcript, an updated resume, the recommendation forms, and a stamped and addressed envelope for each letter. Be sure to clearly mark the deadline on top of the packet.

- Check in a week before your recommendations are due to give people a friendly reminder that the deadline is coming soon.

- Send each of your recommenders a thank-you note to show how much you appreciate the time they've taken to write the letter.

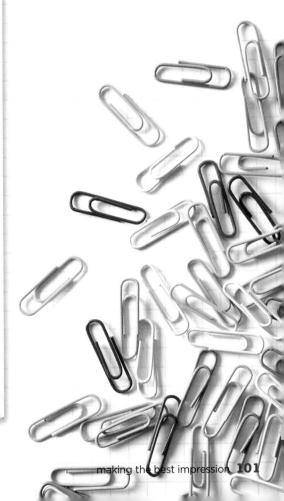

RECOMMENDATION INFO SHEET

Thank you for taking the time to write my college letter of recommendation! The information on this sheet may be helpful. Please let me know if you have any questions.

My recommendation must be submitted no later than: _____

Name: _____

E-mail: _____

GPA: _____

SAT Subject/AP Scores: _____

SAT Scores:_____ ACT Scores:_____

Colleges to which I'm applying: _____
_____
_____

What I hope to study or gain from my college experience: _____
_____
_____

My most meaningful activities and leadership positions: _____
_____
_____

My favorite high school classes and why I enjoyed them:_____
_____
_____

Additional comments and information: _____
_____
_____

interviews

Many schools either offer or require a personal interview. Sometimes they're done on campus by an admissions officer or professor; sometimes alumni volunteers interview students locally around the country. The interview is just as much about giving you the chance to ask questions about the college as is it about giving the college an impression of you.

Be sure to find out if interviews are part of the admissions process at the schools you're applying to and when you should expect to be contacted for one. Then prep for it the same way you would for a job interview. Know enough about the school that you can ask smart questions and show you've put some thought into applying.

17 TIP

Don't send in more than the requested number of recommendations to each school. Admissions officers have tons to read, so if you turn in extras, they may not look at them all and you run the risk that they'll ignore the best ones. (Plus, it kind of makes you look like you don't know how to follow directions.)

17 QUESTIONS AN INTERVIEWER MAY ASK

If you prepare an answer for each of these, chances are you'll be able to handle any question that comes your way. Also, make a mental list of one or two questions that can't be answered just by looking on the school's website. They should be things you really want to know about—interviewers can totally spot insincerity, so be yourself!

1. Why are you interested in this school? _____
_____

2. What classes do you like best?_____
_____

3. What do you plan to study in college? _____
_____

4. What is one of your favorite books, movies, shows, or songs from the past year?_____
_____

5. How would your peers describe you and your personality?
_____
_____

6. What are you passionate about?_____
_____

7. How did you spend the past couple of summers? _____
_____

8. What activities take up most of your time; which is the most enjoyable? _____
_____

9. How do you see yourself having an impact on a college campus?
_____

10. Where do you see yourself in five years? Ten years?
_____
_____

11. What makes you stand out in your school community?

_____

_____

12. How do you feel you've changed since beginning high school?

_____

_____

13. What is your greatest strength? Your greatest weakness?

_____

_____

14. If you could have dinner with one person, living or dead, who would it be? _____

_____

15. What is your most significant accomplishment? _____

_____

16. Describe your family. _____

_____

17. Who do you want to be most proud of you and why? _____

_____

_____

5 Questions
to Ask an Alumni Interviewer

1. Why did you decide to attend your school?

2. What did you like most and least about your college experience?

3. How has your education helped you reach your career goals?

4. What kinds of students do you think benefit most from the educational experience offered at your school?

5. Do you have any advice to offer me?

17 TIP

Practice answering these questions with a friend or family member. Saying your answers out loud is totally different from just going over them in your head.

INTERVIEW CHECKLIST

Follow these steps to make a great impression on interview day!

☐ Confirm the time and location with your interviewer the day before.

☐ Print out directions and make sure you have a reliable way of getting there.

☐ Choose an outfit that you would wear to a nice dinner out with your parents. Show your personality, but don't wear anything that could be considered offensive or too revealing.

☐ Arrive on time (pad in 10 or 15 extra minutes just to be safe, then if you're early, take a walk around the block or use the restroom before checking in).

☐ Have a breath mint *before* the interview (but don't go in there chewing gum!)

☐ Double-check your teeth and makeup in a mirror just beforehand.

☐ Shake the interviewer's hand firmly.

☐ Make eye contact as you talk to him or her.

☐ Ask the interviewer two or three thoughtful questions about the school.

☐ Get contact information from your interviewer and send a thank-you e-mail or note a few days afterward.

When it comes to **affording college**, you just have to believe. Seriously, if you want to go and you've worked hard in high school, you *will* be able to pay for it. Hardly anyone just forks over tens of thousands of dollars in cash—it's all about **loans and grants** and the long-term plan. That doesn't mean you'll definitely be able to afford any college; you'll still have to figure out your family's budget and look at what kind of **financial aid and scholarships** you can get. But the earlier you start looking for the money, the better your chances of finding it.

sticker shock

Most dreams come for a price, whether you're angling for an iPod, a car, or just the most perfect pair of jeans ever. With college, the price can seem overwhelming. The average cost of attending a private or out-of-state public university is about $160,000 for four years, and that doesn't even cover food, books, lab fees, supplies, transportation, or any of the other odds and ends that come up. In many places, that's enough to buy a house or at least a small condo, and few kids or parents have that kind of money lying around. But while the huge number sounds intimidating, it's not like you always have to pay the full price (especially not up front). There's money out there for the taking, in the form of financial aid, grants, and scholarships. You just need to find it. If you're one of the lucky people with parents who've been putting away money for your college fund since the day you were born, you may not need to worry about any of this. But it's still good to know about the costs so you can appreciate how much your parents are handing over and learn how to live on a budget if they cut you off once you get to school.

when to start looking for aid

Juniors should start researching scholarships from organizations, businesses, or annual contests. This is also a good time to get an idea of your family's financial situation. Talk to your parents about how much they think they can afford. To get a realistic idea of how much college will cost, here are all the expenses you should think about, above and beyond tuition.

BOOKS

How much they cost depends on your major (science courses, for example, tend to use huge, expensive text books, while Literature majors can often get away with second-hand paperbacks. Fine Arts, on the other hand, may require fewer books but a lot of art supplies). Just to be safe, estimate that you'll spend anywhere from $1,000-$2,000 per year on books and supplies.

TRANSPORTATION

You'll have to get to and from school, which might mean plane, train, or bus tickets, or gas for commuting. If you live in Portland and want to go to school in Boston, look up average airfares and estimate how many times you'll want to come home during the year. If you plan to commute, first calculate the gas mileage of your car by keeping track of the number of miles you can drive on a full tank of gas. Then divide the cost of a tank of gas by that number. This is the cost of gas per mile. To estimate how much you'll spend in one year of commuting, figure out the number of miles you'll be driving per week, multiply that by the number of weeks in a school year, and multiply that by the cost of gas per mile.

INSURANCE

Most schools offer a medical plan for students, so ask your parents to compare the school plan with your current insurance to decide which gives you the most bang for your buck. If you want to take your car to school out-of-state, talk to your car insurance company to find out the rates for coverage there. If you won't be driving too much, find out the cost for minimal driving coverage and factor that into the budget.

CELL PHONE

You can use your current monthly cost to estimate your yearly expenses, but factor in the possibility that you'll want to up your minutes. If you go to school far away, you might need a bigger plan so you can call home and talk to friends at other schools.

DORM SUPPLIES

The little things add up when you're outfitting a dorm room, but the good news is that you usually only have to buy them once. Check out the **College Shopping List** (page 133) to get an idea of what you'll probably have to buy, and estimate an amount for the **College Budget Worksheet** (page 110).

ENTERTAINMENT AND PERSONAL EXPENSES

Keep track of your expenses for two months—that means movies, music downloads, magazine subscriptions, pedicures, haircut/color, shopping, eating out, coffee runs, concerts, and anything else you spend money on. Multiply that amount by six to get an estimated total for one year. If you plan to go to school in a city where things are more expensive than in your hometown, add a few hundred dollars to your total.

Just keep in mind that your social life may change once you start school—you might never go out to the movies, even though you went once a week in high school. Or you might decide that eating out with friends isn't as important when you can just go to the dining hall together. Instead, you may want to spend your money on new things like sorority dues or road trips. Think of this as just a rough guide.

myth I'll never be able to afford a private or out-of-state university.

truth Sometimes, because of large endowments, private schools can offer even more financial aid than public schools. And with the help of scholarships and loans, you can make an out-of-state college doable.

COLLEGE BUDGET WORKSHEET

Use this sheet to estimate how much you and your parents can expect to spend on college per year, before factoring in financial aid.

Tuition $ _____

Room and Board $ _____

Books $ _____

Transportation $ _____

Insurance $ _____

Cell Phone $ _____

Dorm Supplies $ _____

Entertainment $ _____

Personal Expenses $_____

TOTAL $ _____

types of financial aid

Financial aid is available at all colleges and universities to help with the cost of tuition, room and board, fees, and other expenses. While each school has a different method for deciding whether a student is eligible, the types of aid offered are pretty much the same.

NEED-BASED AID

Need-based aid is money that you can get based on how much you need it, rather than on how good your grades are or whether you won an award or contest. It can come from the state and federal governments, as well as the college itself. Schools use a combination of their own application, the Free Application for Federal Student Aid (FAFSA), and the College Scholarship Service Profile (CSS Profile) to help them determine how much money your family can afford to pay for college, and therefore how much you can get in aid. (You'll find more info about each of these applications later on in this chapter.) Unless you're an emancipated minor, the amount you get is based on both your income and savings and your parents', and can be given in the form of grants, scholarships, loans, and work-study pay.

Grants and scholarships

are the best type of need-based aid you can get because you don't have to pay taxes on the money and you don't have to repay it. Whatever amount you receive in grant and scholarship money will be automatically deducted from your tuition bill. Grant money is typically doled out by the government or college, while scholarships are often awarded by colleges or organizations based on a performance of some kind, say, in the area of academics, athletics, the arts, or a winning essay.

Loans have to be

repaid. However, most government-based education loans are offered at low interest rates and don't start collecting interest until you leave college or graduate. If you receive loans as part of your financial aid package, the lender will pay that amount each year and it will be deducted from your tuition.

Work-study is

money that a college pays you for working at a part-time job on campus.

TYPES OF GOVERNMENT FINANCIAL AID

Federal Pell Grant
Given to students with the greatest need, based on information from the FAFSA. Anyone whose income falls within a certain range determined by the government each year receives this grant.

Federal Supplemental Educational Opportunity Grant
Students who are eligible for the Federal Pell Grant may also receive this additional grant from a college.

State Grant
Given to students mostly based on need, but sometimes merit (good grades, etc.). You usually have to go to a school in the same state that gives you the grant in order to use it.

Federal Perkins Loan
Given only to students who show a need. The interest doesn't start adding on and you don't have to start paying it back until after you leave school.

Federal Subsidized Loan (Stafford)
Given only to students who show a need. The government pays the interest on these loans as long as you're enrolled in college. You don't have to start repaying them until six months after graduation or leaving school.

Federal Unsubsidized Loan (Stafford)
You don't have to demonstrate need on the FAFSA to qualify for an unsubsidized Stafford Loan—any eligible student may apply. Interest does start adding on immediately, although you don't have to pay it back until after college if you don't want to.

MERIT-BASED AID

Merit-based aid is usually given in the form of a grant or scholarship that you don't have to repay, either from the school or an outside organization. You can get one based on your academic performance, athletic ability, race or ethnicity, artistic talent, or some other asset you bring to a college or community. For more info on merit-based aid check out the scholarship websites in the **Resources** section (page 138).

applying for need-based aid

FREE APPLICATION FOR FEDERAL STUDENT AID (FAFSA)

how it works

To know if you qualify for need-based financial aid, you and your family have to fill out the **Free Application for Federal Student Aid (FAFSA)**. This is a government form that estimates a family's ability to pay for college based on information like the previous year's income, assets, savings, and available cash. You can submit the FAFSA as early as January 1 for the following academic year, and it's best to do it as soon as you can so you'll know what kind of money you're dealing with. Check with each of your schools to find out their deadlines for turning in the form. You can list up to six colleges to receive a copy of your report when you first fill out the FAFSA, and you can add additional schools once your information has been processed.

what you need to fill out the application

The FAFSA is available online (see **Resources,** page 138). You and your parents will need to have the following information on hand to complete it:

- Most recent federal tax forms
- Record of prior year earnings
- Record of any nontaxable income
- Current bank statements
- Record of business, farm, stocks, bonds, and other investments

If when you are completing the FAFSA your family's most current year's tax returns are not yet available, don't let that make you miss your deadlines. Go ahead and file it anyway by estimating the numbers using last year's tax returns.

A few weeks after you submit your FAFSA, a Student Aid Report (SAR) will be sent to you. This is a copy of all the information you originally included on your FAFSA. Review it carefully and make any corrections or add your latest tax figures if you need to. If your family's tax info still is not available by the time schools are ready to send your financial aid packages, they may send you an estimate of financial aid that will become final once you get them the updated numbers. If you need to make corrections to your SAR, you can send the paperwork back to the processing center or file your changes electronically. To do this, you'll need to register for a personal identification number (PIN) from the Department of Education. visit the Federal Student Aid's Web site (www.pin.ed.gov,) and select "Apply for a Pin." If you don't have any corrections, you're done—the schools you listed will all receive a copy of the information. Once you're in college, you'll need to update the FAFSA annually in order to keep receiving financial aid.

estimated family contribution (EFC)

The purpose of filling out the FAFSA is to determine how much money you and your family can contribute to college. This amount is called your **Estimated Family Contribution (EFC)**, which is divided into the expected *parent* contribution and expected *student* contribution. The expected student contribution is based on any financial assets you have and what you can earn over the summer and during the school year. The parent portion of the EFC is based on annual income, assets, and savings that can be put toward college.

If the FAFSA determines that your EFC is $17,000, then no matter what the cost of where you apply, schools will know that your family can only contribute $17,000 that year toward college. Once your EFC has been determined, it's subtracted from the total cost of attending your college. (The cost of attending includes tuition, room and board, books, supplies, fees, and travel expenses for one year.) The difference equals your family's financial need.

Just because the FAFSA determines your EFC is X amount, doesn't necessarily mean that the school you want to go to will be able to make up the whole difference in your financial aid package. Every college handles financial aid differently, so you'll need to do some research to figure out whether a particular school is likely to meet your needs. The financial aid questionnaire at the end of this chapter lists important questions to ask each admissions office.

THE COLLEGE SCHOLARSHIP SERVICE (CSS) PROFILE

The College Scholarship Service Profile is yet another form—this one's often required by private colleges and scholarship programs. It asks more detailed questions about your family's financial situation. If the CSS Profile is required by the universities to which you're applying, you'll need to register either by phone or online and pay a processing fee, which varies depending on how many colleges you need to send your CSS profile to. You can get paper registration forms in your guidance office or from college financial aid offices starting on September 1 for the following academic year. Online forms are available at www.college-board.com/profile.html. Check with each school to find out their deadline for submitting the CSS.

INSTITUTIONAL APPLICATIONS

In addition to the FAFSA and CSS Profile, some schools also require a form of their own, which—again!—provides *more* detailed information to help that school determine the amount of financial aid to offer you. Many schools give merit-based scholarships that require a separate application. Be sure to research all the scholarship opportunities at each school you apply to and see if you meet the basic requirements for consideration. That might include a certain GPA or major; a particular ethnic, religious, or cultural background; a special athletic, musical, or artistic talent; or being the child of a parent or grandparent who attended that school (also called being a "legacy"). You may have to write another essay in order to be considered, but a few more hours of writing will definitely be worth the thousands of dollars in aid you might get out of it!

APPLYING TO INTERNATIONAL UNIVERSITIES

Financial aid is available at schools outside the U.S., but every university has a different policy about how it's given out. The best thing to do is visit the financial aid websites of the schools you're interested in and request more info. Be sure you read the instructions carefully and note the deadlines. Late applications seriously lower your chances of getting the best package. (For websites with useful information about financial aid at foreign schools, see **Resources**, page 138.)

applying for merit-based aid

There are thousands of merit-based scholarships out there. Just by taking the PSAT/NMSQT, you put yourself in the running for a National Merit or Achievement Scholarship. At some schools being a National Merit or Achievement Scholar can even get you a full-tuition scholarship. While this is one of the best-known programs, there are lots more based on different criteria, like gender, race, religion, nationality, state or city of birth, GPA, athletic ability, school spirit, leadership, community service, excellence in math and science, intended major, intended career...the list goes on! For websites with up-to-date info on scholarship opportunities, see **Resources**, page 138).

Once you start receiving scholarships, you're required to let colleges know about any outside aid money you receive. Each school handles this info differently. Some will reduce the amount of money you're eligible to get from the college; others will put the money toward your student loans. Some will reduce the amount of money you're expected to pay out of pocket (counting the scholarship money as part of your contribution). Many schools will do a combo of all these things. Before you make your final decision about where to go, check with the financial aid offices of each school to find out how your outside grants or scholarships will affect your situation.

weighing the cost

Applying for financial aid can be an intimidating and confusing process. It means dealing with lots of forms and tax returns and parent signatures, all of which can be a huge pain. But if you put in the time, it should pay off in the form of thick financial aid packages in your mailbox, and you'll have more options about where you can afford to go. A few last do's and don'ts:

DO make sure you read all the directions for each school carefully! Most ask for standard information; but some of your schools might require additional or different material.

DO take note of all the deadlines. Note whether they're "receive by" dates or "postmark" dates, and be sure to mail or complete the online applications by or before the dates they need to be received.

DON'T forget to make or print out copies of all the forms you complete. If one of the schools notifies you that information is missing, you'll be glad you have a copy on hand

to fax back or resubmit so you won't have to fill it out from scratch. If you don't get any notice that a school received your forms, call the financial aid office to check.

DO put the cost of college into perspective. College is one of the best investments you'll ever make—it opens up greater job opportunities and gives you the skills to impress employers. This is one case where going into debt isn't such a bad thing. There are even some career fields, like teaching, that may offer to repay your student loans if you accept job offers in certain underserved

areas. And student loan companies are good about providing low-interest rates and payment plans that work with your budget after graduation.

DON'T let money problems prevent you from achieving your goals. Do what you can ahead of time to start saving for college. Write out a budget for saving over the summer and school year. Vow to save a certain percentage of your part-time job money in a college fund. Apply for every scholarship you can. If you start early and do the research, you can get around almost any financial problem.

FINANCIAL AID QUESTIONNAIRE

TAKE THIS WITH YOU!

Here are ten questions you should ask the college admissions office at each school to which you apply. Make copies of this form and take it along with you on your campus visits.

NAME OF SCHOOL _____

1. What is the total cost of attendance?
   _____
   _____

2. Does applying for financial aid factor into the admissions decision?
   _____
   _____

3. What factors outside of financial resources determine a student's financial aid package (i.e., grades, test scores, class rank)?
   _____
   _____

4. Will the college or university meet my full or partial need as determined by the FAFSA?
   _____
   _____

5. Are there scholarships or grants available based on merit, and what are the requirements for consideration?
   _____
   _____

6. Is outside scholarship or grant money used to replace aid in the college financial aid package?
   _____
   _____

7. What kind of work-study opportunities are available on campus?
   _____
   _____

8. Is financial aid guaranteed for all years of attendance?
   _____
   _____

9. Does a student need to maintain a certain GPA in order to receive financial aid?
   _____
   _____

10. Will the university match other schools' offers of financial aid?
    _____
    _____

O kay, so it's the summer before your senior year, and that means **crunch time**. You'll want to **get started** as early as you can, since applying to college is going to be a ton of work on top of your classes and other commitments.

the short list

Finish up all your college research by the end of summer or early fall of senior year, so you can narrow your bigger list down to the eight or ten schools to which you'll ultimately apply.

Those eight or ten schools should represent a good mix. The majority should be **competitive schools**. That means you've checked the GPA and testing stats on last year's class of freshmen, and you fall above or in the upper half of the average range. If you've got your heart set on a couple of **dream schools**, go ahead and apply. Sure, the odds may be against you, but then again, you might just be exactly what they're looking for! When asked what they would do differently if they could, many students say they'd take a risk and apply to schools that they really liked but thought were too hard to get into.

At least one or two of the colleges on your short list should be **safety schools**—places where you know beyond a shadow of a doubt that you can get in because your stats are well above those of the average admitted student, or the school offers guaranteed admission for students with a certain GPA, class rank, or state of residence. Safety schools should still be places you want to go though—they should meet the must-have criteria on your college checklist just like your other picks.

Find out all the deadlines and requirements for each school and write them in your calendar. Some will offer early admissions programs or have a separate deadline for people who want to apply for merit or athletic scholarships, so make a note of that if you're one of them. Use **The Short List**, on the next page, to keep track of everything you need for each school's application.

THE SHORT LIST

Here's where you can keep track of all the deadlines and materials you need to apply to each school. If you're applying to more than ten schools, make a copy of this form and keep it in the folder at the start of this chapter.

	EXAMPLE	1	2	3	4	5	6	7	8	9	10
School	Reed College										
Application Deposit Due Date	1/15										
Application Deposit Submitted	✓										
Application Due Date	1/15										
Application Received	✓										
Testing Required ACT	either										
SAT	either										
SAT II	optional										
Last Testing Date Accepted											
Requested Transcript & Counselor Recommendation											
Reported Test Scores ACT	✓										
SAT	✓										
SAT II											
Requested Teacher Recommendations	✓										

	EXAMPLE	1	2	3	4	5	6	7	8	9	10
School	Reed College										
Essays Completed	✓										
Application Completed											
Proofread											
Make Photocopies of Application											
Application Submitted!											
FAFSA Submitted (Make Copies)											
CSS Profile Submitted (Make Copies)											
School Fin. Aid Forms Submitted (Make Copies)											

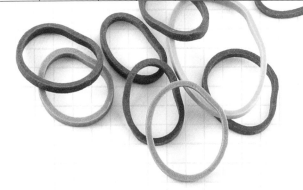

types of admission

EARLY ADMISSIONS

Some schools offer an early admissions program, which lets you apply earlier than the regular admission deadline and find out sooner whether or not you got in. The two main types of early admission are early action and early decision. The main difference between these is that early decision is binding—**that means you can apply to only one school for early decision**. If you get in, you have to withdraw all your other applications and agree to attend that school. Early decision isn't for everyone, but it has its advantages. If you're *sure* of your first-choice school, it means you'll be competing against fewer applicants than you would during the regular decision process. Early action, on the other hand, is a sort of middle ground. It's nonbinding, so you'll still find out sooner whether or not you're admitted, but if you are, you can still choose to go to another school. These deadlines are typically in the fall (mid-October to mid-November), but the specific dates vary by institution.

REGULAR ADMISSIONS

Regular admissions deadlines are usually somewhere between mid-December and mid-February. Acceptance letters usually come in the spring, and you typically have about a month after getting them to make your decision and tell schools whether or not you'll be attending.

ROLLING ADMISSIONS

Some schools offer "rolling admission," which means that there's no official deadline for submitting your application. About two months after you've applied (whenever that might be), you'll find out if you're being admitted. These schools keep enrolling students throughout the year until they've either filled all their spots or are no longer accepting applications for that year. Keep in mind that financial aid and housing is typically decided on a first-come, first-served basis, so if you need money or a dorm room, don't wait until the last minute to apply.

17 TIP

Many schools use the Common Application, which is a single application that you can submit to multiple colleges. This can be a huge timesaver, but sometimes schools also require you to send a supplement to the Common Application that asks questions unique to that school. Make sure you've gathered all the necessary forms before you start applying.

fall of senior year time line

✔ **Make your short list:** Narrow down your list of schools to eight or ten choices and decide whether or not you'll apply early anywhere.

✔ **Report test scores and sign up for fall test dates:** Make sure you've taken all the tests required by each school and sign up for any additional tests before your application deadlines.

✔ **Meet with your guidance counselor:** Schedule a meeting with your guidance counselor at least a month before the first application deadline. Bring all of your counselor recommendation forms, transcript requests, and stamped and addressed envelopes for returning the information to the school. Go over all the schools to which you want to apply and be sure your counselor

knows everything you need from her and when you need it by.

✔ **Meet with teachers:** Set up meetings with each teacher who'll be writing a recommendation letter for you. Give them a copy of the **Recommendation Info Sheet** (see page 102), the list of schools to which you're applying, their deadlines for receiving recommendations, and addressed and stamped envelopes for each letter.

✔ **Brainstorm essay topics:** Start brainstorming possible essay topics as soon as the current year's applications are available.

✔ **Tell your story:** By now you've spent a lot of time getting to know yourself: your strengths, talents, abilities, and passions. You know what sets you apart, and you've picked schools

that will help you develop your interests. Now it's time to convince each college that you're a great fit for their campus.

✔ **Gather extra materials:** If you have special talents that you think aren't captured in your application, check with school admissions offices to see whether they'll accept supplemental materials, and what kinds of materials are okay. If allowed, now's the time to put together your demo CD (for musicians), slides or an art portfolio (for fine artists), a performance DVD (for actresses/dancers), scientific research or an abstract (for scientists), or a recruiting video (for athletes). Send copies, not originals, since chances are you won't get them back.

✔ **Proofread your entire application:** Make sure

you've answered all the questions and filled it out completely. Don't rely on your computer's spell-check—it won't catch correctly spelled words that are used in the wrong way. Have someone you trust read over your work. Double-check that your essays and short answers mention the right school for each application, so that you don't end up telling Boston University how much you love Duke.

✔ **Make copies:** Photocopy all your paper applications and print out online ones. You'll want to have a record of the information just in case something goes missing a few weeks into the review process. Keep a file for each college to which you apply, so that it's easier to find stuff when you need it.

✔ **Submit!** Once your applications are completed and you're satisfied with the results, it's time to mail or hit send. Give yourself a deadline that's a few days or weeks before the school's actual deadline. That way you can stress out about finishing by your own deadline, then relax and have a few extra days to look everything over before the real cut-off. If you wait until the last minute, you might end up rushing and making mistakes that you would have caught if you had more time.

lady-in-waiting

Okay, so your applications are submitted and there's nothing left to do except wait, right? That's mostly true, but there are a couple of things to keep in mind while you're waiting for those acceptance letters to start rolling in.

COMPLETE YOUR FINANCIAL AID FORMS

If you're applying for financial aid, there's probably still some work to be done. Because financial aid deadlines typically fall after application deadlines review the info in chapter eight.

COMBAT SENIORITIS

Just because you've turned in your applications doesn't mean that your grades no longer count. Schools will be checking midyear report cards as they make their decisions, so it's important to keep doing your best.

STAY IN THE PRESENT

It's fine to relax and enjoy your senior year; you've worked hard and deserve a break! But there are still a few more months of high school life to enjoy. Don't let your excitement about the future make you miss out on all the end-of-year fun.

getting your responses

You've finally made it to the crazy, nerve-wracking moment when you find out the possibilities for the next four years of your life. It could all work out exactly the way you planned, or you might have to rethink things if your top choices don't pan out.

Most schools now post admission decisions online, and you'll get one of four answers: You'll either be admitted, denied, deferred (if you're applying early), or waitlisted. If you're admitted—yay!—the next move is up to you. (Unless you applied early decision—then you *must* enroll.) Everybody else can decide to enroll then and there or wait to make a decision until they hear back from other schools. Check with each school's admissions office to find out when you have to decide and send in your tuition deposit.

DEFERRED: WHAT DOES IT REALLY MEAN?

Getting deferred during early admission is like your crush saying, "Let's just be friends for now." Definitely not the answer you were looking for. You put yourself out there, told the school they're your number one, and now they want to "get to know you better first." Ugh! But deferment isn't actually code for rejection like it might be with your crush (who, by the way, isn't good enough for you anyway). Getting deferred means the school likes you—a lot—but they need to answer some questions about your application before they can make a final decision. There are a few reasons why you might get deferred, such as:

• Your application is incomplete. Rather than flat-out denying you, the school's giving you a chance to finish submitting all the requested materials.

• Your grades are a little all-over-the-place, and the admissions office wants to consider your midyear report card before making a decision. This means you have a chance to really wow the college with stellar marks during your senior year.

• Your test scores aren't as high as they could be, so they're giving you the chance to retake the tests and raise your scores in time for regular admissions.

Remember that you won't actually get to find out which of these situations may apply to you. So, if you get a deferral letter, talk to the admissions office and find out if there's anything you can do to help them make their decision. If you still really want to go there, send them a letter saying so and update them on any new accomplishments, leadership positions, test scores, or awards you've received since submitting your application.

REJECTION

Getting rejected is never easy, and it almost makes it worse when people say things like "look on the bright side" or "it could be worse" or "it wasn't meant to be." Sure, all those things might be true, but when you're still reeling from the disappointment, sometimes you just want to feel disappointed. And that's fine.

The important thing is to not take a rejection letter personally. Colleges have become increasingly hard to get into over the years because more and more students are applying, but the number of spots isn't increasing at the same rate. As awful as rejection is, it's a part of life that we all have to deal with at some point. And once you get over the initial let-down of not getting into your favorite school(s), it's time to think about other steps you can take to reach your goals.

If you've applied to a wide variety of colleges (including some safety schools), then you should have some other good offers on the table. Think about what it is you liked about your favorite school and choose one that has the most similar attributes. Remember: If it doesn't turn out to be everything you hoped for, you can always transfer your sophomore year. If you're really not happy with your other options, you might even want to think about taking a year off to travel abroad or work, and then reapply to schools next year. Maybe attending community college for a year or two is a good choice if you want to save some money while racking up a few prerequisites, then earn your degree at a four-year school once you've picked a major. Whatever you decide, it's important to make the most of your experience, since if you do decide to transfer or reapply, schools will want to see what you did during your year off or while enrolled at another college.

WAIT... I'VE BEEN WAITLISTED!

There are always more qualified students applying than there are spots available, so a college or university will often create a waitlist of people they'd like to admit if they had the space. That way, if some of the students who were accepted decide to go somewhere else, the school can start sending offers to people on that list.

If you get a waitlist letter, take it as a compliment. It means the school really does think you'd be a great asset to the campus; they just don't have enough room. If you want to remain on the waitlist and hope for a spot to open up, you need to let the school know. *But you also need to accept an offer of admission at another school, just in case that potential spot never becomes a reality.*

The number of students put on the waitlist varies at every school, and the number (if any) of those who eventually get admitted depends on how many students accept their initial offer of admission. You may find out as early as May or as late as August whether you'll get a spot, so it's important to get fully on board with an alternative school in case the waitlist doesn't pan out.

FINAL ANSWER

Once you've got your acceptances, you may know right away where you want to go. But if you're having a hard time deciding between schools, go back to your list of must-haves and compare your choices. Lots of schools offer a prospective students weekend, which is a chance for you to visit the campus, meet other admitted students, stay in a dorm, and sit in on classes. Visiting campus while school is in session could help sway you one way or the other. If financial aid is a big consideration, comparing the packages offered by each school could also be a deciding factor.

If you really have your heart set on a school but the cost is just out of reach, contact the financial aid office and talk about your options. Let them know if your family's financial situation has changed since you turned in your application—they'll take that into account to adjust your aid package.

Once you've been admitted, the tables are turned—now the schools are waiting to find out whether *you'll* accept or reject *them!* When you decide where to go, make sure you fill out all the necessary forms and send in a deposit, if it's required to hold your place. It's also a nice courtesy to let the other schools that offered you admission know where you'll be going in the fall. Now it's really time to relax and enjoy the rest of your senior year!

myth The financial aid package I get is set in stone.

truth Schools do have wiggle room to adjust the package under certain circumstances. If you've already been admitted, that means the school wants you and should do what they can to help get you there!

college comparison chart

Use this chart to keep track of and compare the decisions and financial aid packages you receive from each college.

SCHOOL	ADMISSIONS DECISION	GRANTS/ SCHOLARSHIPS	LOANS	WORK-STUDY	PARENT CONTRIBUTION	STUDENT CONTRIBUTION
1.						
2.						
3.						
4.						
5.						
6.						
7.						
8.						
9.						
10.						

Congratulations! A major chapter in your life is about to end, and a brand-new, crazy, exciting one is about to start. There are some **really amazing times** ahead, but before you even head off to campus, there's one more thing to do—**go shopping!** Here's a list of some not-so-obvious things you might want to add to your usual back-to-school spree.

COLLEGE SHOPPING LIST

☐ **BATHROBE**—Invest in a cute, comfy one for those hallway treks to the shower (you can't really get away with your usual cami and undies in a coed dorm!).

☐ **SHOWER CADDY**—You can't keep all your shampoo and stuff in a communal bathroom (well, you can, but it'll disappear a lot faster than usual), so you'll need something to haul it all back and forth in.

☐ **SPILLPROOF TRAVEL MUG**—Some dining halls use paper everything; since you'll be eating there up to three times a day, a reusable mug is a little more environmentally friendly.

☐ **SPARE FLIP-FLOPS**—You don't want to shower barefoot in the same stall where hundreds if not thousands of strange feet have tread before you.

☐ **MINI READING LIGHT**—This gives you the option to stay up late without annoying your sleeping roommate, who somehow manages to get her work done before 3 a.m.

☐ **EXTRA-LONG TWIN SHEETS**—Most colleges use "extra-long" mattresses (don't worry—plenty of cute sheets come in this size). But double-check with your residence hall to be sure.

☐ **EGG-CRATE MATTRESS PAD**—Make your new dorm bed as comfy as home by bringing along an extra bit of cushion.

☐ **MINI FRIDGE**—You can keep fruit, veggies, and cold drinks right in your room so you won't always have to go all the way to the dining hall.

☐ **KITCHEN STORAGE CONTAINERS**—Bring them to the cafeteria and stock up on leftovers, and use them as surrogate dishes when you need a bowl for your cereal.

☐ **EXTERNAL HARD DRIVE**—Invest in a large one and backup your computer weekly so you never lose your projects.

☐ **DRY-ERASE MESSAGE BOARD**—It comes in handy for exchanging funny (and occasionally useful) messages with roomies or hallmates.

☐ **POP-UP LAUNDRY HAMPER**—This little gizmo folds up conveniently to save space when your stuff's all clean.

☐ **EXTENSION CORDS/ POWER STRIP**—Otherwise you might end up with just one outlet for your 37 electronic devices.

☐ **MINI TOOL KIT**—You'll need it to put together your loft and to hang up your requisite John Belushi "COLLEGE" poster. Plus, you never realize how many fix-it jobs crop up over the course of a year until your dad isn't there to fix it.

☐ **MINI DIGITAL VOICE RECORDER**—If you're not a licensed stenographer, ensure you don't miss any of those lecture notes.

☐ **EXTRA HANGERS**—The few misshapen wire ones left by last year's resident aren't going to cut it.

☐ **IRON AND MINI IRONING BOARD**—Even if you're wearing jeans and t-shirts every day, you can still look nice!

before you go

If there's one single thing we hope you've gotten from this book, it's the importance of knowing who you are and having the confidence to be true to yourself in any situation. As you get ready to head off to college, think back on the last four years. The person you were in high school helped get you into college, and you should be proud of that. But once you arrive on campus, the slate is wiped clean. You're in a new environment with professors and classmates who have no idea who you are or what you have to offer. Now you get to decide who to be in this next phase of your life, and what you want out of your college experience. Here are some final tips to take with you:

- Take a lighter load your first semester or quarter of school so that you can adjust to (and enjoy!) your new environment.

- Get involved in a few activities freshman year to find a small community of friends within the larger college campus.

- Balance required courses with electives to explore potential majors.

- Stay healthy with good nutrition and exercise. Be sure to take advantage of your school's gym and intramural sports—you'll never get these things for free again!

- Understand the required credits and classes you have to complete in order to graduate on time.

- Practice good time management. You parents may have always been around to remind you of important dates and deadlines, but now that you're on your own you'll want to invest in a planner.

- Get to know your professors by meeting with them during their office hours (the times of day outside of class that they set aside to be available for students to drop by). It's a good way to learn about research opportunities, and

becoming friendly with them could be especially helpful if you end up applying to graduate school programs.

- Stick to a budget and avoid racking up credit card debt. With credit card companies sending more and more offers to college students, it's become a big problem. Only paying the minimums or failing to pay on time can damage your credit score for a *long* time—like decades.

- Take advantage of your college career center to find out about summer internship and potential fellowship opportunities.

Now all you have left to do is pack your bags, say your good-byes, and get excited about the next four years of your life. Look at everything you've accomplished, and pat yourself on the back. Surviving high school, getting a better understanding of yourself, putting all the effort into applying to college, getting into schools, and deciding where to go—you did it all! So whenever you're feeling overwhelmed, confused, stressed, or worried about your future, take a deep breath and think about everything you've already achieved. Be inspired by your past and remind yourself that in the future, you can do anything you set your mind to. Good luck!

glossary

ACT: originally known as the American College Testing program, the ACT is a set of four multiple-choice tests (five, if you take the optional writing test), and it covers English, math, reading, and science. The ACT is one of the standardized tests required for admission to many colleges and universities.

Associate Degree: the degree that you'll receive after completing the requirements of a two-year college, usually referred to as community colleges or JCs (Junior Colleges). Once you receive your associate degree, you can transfer to a four-year college where your associate degree credits will be applied toward your bachelor's degree.

Bachelor's Degree (BA or BS): a Bachelor of Arts or Bachelor of Sciences is the academic degree that you receive once you've completed all the requirements for the college or university you attend. That usually takes four years, but some students may graduate in as few as three years while others may take five or more.

College Scholarship Service (CSS) Profile: the financial aid application service of The College Board, required by many universities in order to be considered for financial aid.

Common Application: a single application that can be submitted to multiple schools.

Doctorate: the highest degree that you can receive from a graduate program.

Early Action: a standard nonbinding early admission plan that notifies the student of her admission decision well in advance of the regular decision notification. Students can apply to multiple schools under early action and are not required to make a decision on where they will attend until the spring deadline.

Early Decision: a binding early admission plan under which a student may only apply to one school early. If admitted and offered an acceptable financial aid package, the student must commit to attend and withdraw all regular applications to other schools. Early decision applications are usually due in November and students are typically notified before the end of the year.

Extracurriculars: activities in which a student might participate outside of the requirements of her high school.

Free Application for Federal Student Aid (FAFSA): a government financial aid form that estimates a family's ability to pay for college based on information such as the previous year's income, assets, savings, and available cash. The information collected on the FAFSA determines whether you qualify for federal, state, and institutional aid in the form of grants, scholarships, loans, and work-study.

GPA: stands for grade point average and is one of the main factors a college considers in the application process.

Graduate Schools: schools that offer advanced degrees beyond the bachelor such as masters or doctorates.

Greek Life: the fraternities and sororities that make up the Greek system of a college or university. They can be social, service, or professional organizations where members often live together, and are known for social events, charitable outreach, and alumni networking.

Ivy League: A group of schools including Brown, Columbia, Cornell, Dartmouth, Harvard, Princeton, University of Pennsylvania, and Yale. The term was originally used to refer to eight members of an athletic league; now these schools are considered to be academically prestigious and highly selective.

Liberal arts: traditional and general education in subjects such as literature, history, mathematics, natural science, social science, language, art, and music.

Masters Degree: an academic degree typically earned after fulfilling at least one year of requirements beyond the bachelor's degree. Many people choose to get a Master's in a particular area of study because it indicates advanced training and coursework, which is helpful when applying for certain jobs.

National Merit and Achievement Scholarships: scholarships based on performance on the PSAT/NMSQT and SAT, awarded annually to over 8,000 students. Scholarships are provided by the National Merit Program, corporate sponsors, and colleges.

PLAN: a practice ACT test typically administered in the fall of 10th grade.

PSAT/NMSQT: stands for Preliminary SAT and National Merit Qualifying Test—a practice SAT typically taken in the fall of junior year. Junior year scores count toward qualifying students for National Merit Scholarships. The PSAT/NMSQT may also be taken prior to junior year for practice.

Professional Schools: graduate schools that offer advanced degrees in fields such as dentistry, law, or medicine.

SAT: stands for Scholastic Assessment Test, one of the standardized tests required for admission to many colleges and universities. It's comprised of three main sections: critical reading, math, and writing.

Scholarship: a gift of money to be used toward education.

TA: stands for teacher's assistant; usually a graduate student who teaches or assists in the teaching of undergraduate classes, labs, or discussion sections.

Transcript: a copy of a student's academic record; admissions officers rely on transcripts to evaluate a student's high school academic performance.

Undergraduate: a college or university student who hasn't yet received a bachelor's degree.

Waitlist: a list of qualified applicants compiled by a college or university who may eventually be admitted if space at the school becomes available.

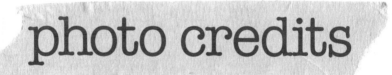

photo credits

iStockphoto: 25, 27, 30, 37, 49, 59, 73, 74, 79, 101, 110, 123
Kate Mathis: 108-109; 113-116
Garry McLeod: 131
Punchstock: Chapter Openers 2, 3, 4, 6, 8; pages 11, 33, 41, 60, 77, 106, 125
Kelly Roberts: 19, 26, 50, 55, 118, 124, 131
Todd Selby: Chapter 7 Opener
Jason Todd: Chapter Openers 1, 9, 10; pages 20, 23, 64
PhotoAlto Photography/Veer: Chapter 5 Opener

resources

COLLEGE SEARCH WEBSITES:
American Association of Community Colleges: www.aacc.nche.edu
Association of Jesuit Colleges and Universities: www.ajcunet.edu/
Campus Dirt: www.campusdirt.com
Christian College Mentor: www.christiancollegementor.org/
College Confidential: www.collegeconfidential.com
The Common Application: www.commonapp.org
eCampus Tours: www.ecampustours.com
HBCUMentor: www.hbcumentor.org (historically black colleges)
Hillel—The Foundation for Jewish Campus Life: www.hillel.org
The National Catholic College Admission Association: www.catholiccollegesonline.org/
Peterson's Guide: www.petersons.com
TheU: www.theu.com
US News & World Report Education Section:
www.usnews.com/sections/education/index.html
The Women's College Coalition: www.womenscolleges.org
Xap: www.xap.com

COLLEGE COUNSELING AND TUTORING WEBSITES:
College Match: www.collegematchus.com
KnowHow2Go: www.knowhow2go.org
National Association for College Admission Counseling: www.nacacnet.org
Sylvan Learning Centers: www.educate.com
Ventures Scholars Program: www.venturescholar.org

ACTIVITIES AND INVOLVEMENT
AmeriCorps: www.americorps.gov
American Jewish World Service: www.ajws.org
Global Crossroad: www.globalcrossroad.com
NCAA: www.ncaa.org (athletics)
Rock the Vote: www.rockthevote.com
Volunteer Adventures: www.volunteeradventures.com
Young Adult Library Services Association www.ala.org/ala/yalsa (outside reading)
Youthnoise: www.youthnoise.com

STANDARDIZED TESTING HELP:
ACT/PLAN: www.act.org
Education Testing Services (ETS): www.ets.org
FairTest: The National Center for Fair and Open Testing: www.fairtest.org
International Baccalaureate: www.ibo.org
Kaplan: www.kaplan.com
Princeton Review: www.princetonreview.com
SAT/PSAT/AP: www.collegeboard.com

FINANCIAL AID AND SCHOLARSHIPS:
CollegeNET: www.collegenet.com
College Scholarship Service (CSS) Profile: https://profileonline.collegeboard.com/
The Education Resources Institute—TERi College Access: www.tericollegeaccess.org
EduPASS: www.edupass.org/finaid/ (for foreign students)
Expected Family Contribution Calculator
https://apps.collegeboard.com/fincalc/servlet/efcCalculatorServlet
FastWeb!: www.fastweb.com
FinAid!: www.finaid.org
Free Application for Financial Aid (FAFSA): www.fafsa.ed.gov
Gates Millennium Scholars: www.gmsp.org
International Education Financial Aid: www.iefa.org (for study abroad))
National Merit Scholarship Corporation: www.nationalmerit.org
Scholarship America: www.scholarshipamerica.org
The Scholarship Coach: www.scholarshipcoach.com
United Negro College Fund: www.uncf.org

SEVENTEEN: www.seventeen.com/college-career
At seventeen.com, you'll find expert answers to your biggest college questions, test-taking tips to improve your scores, scholarship listings, and a searchable database to find out anything you ever wanted to know about any college!

index

JAYE J. FENDERSON

Jaye attended Columbia University where she received a Bachelor of Arts in English and French. After college, she worked as a senior admission officer at Columbia University, and it was there that Jaye recognized a need for greater awareness about the college admission process and decided to use the medium of entertainment to educate students and families about what it takes to get into college.

In 2005, Jaye co-created and produced ABC's The Scholar, an unscripted television drama that gave 10 high school seniors the chance to compete for a full ride college scholarship. Jaye is currently in production as producer and director of the feature-length documentary film First Generation which takes a thought provoking look at the state of equal opportunity in education by chronicling the lives of low-income high school students who are first in their family attempting to attend college.

Jaye is a volunteer college counselor with the non-profit organization College Summit and a consultant for the Seattle-based college placement firm College Match. She has 8 years of film and television experience directing documentary-style interviews, producing television shows and short films, and casting such shows as 30 Days, Laguna Beach: The Real OC, The Simple Life, and Moves. Jaye has been interviewed by USA Today, US News & World Report, The Chronicle of Higher Education, and Inside Higher Ed. She has published numerous articles on college admission, is a monthly contributor to the professional women's forum Damsels in Success, and since 2005 has been a college advice columnist for Seventeen.com. This is her first book.

For more information about Jaye and her latest projects visit: www.ironstrings.com